WHAT DOES LAW MEAN, MUMU?

First Published in Ireland in 2020
ISBN 978-1-9163730-0-6

Porteo Marketing
Seaforth Lodge
Glenageary
County Dublin
www.porteomarketing.com
+353 (0) 284 7960
paulynmarrinan@outlook.com

Layout by Three Rock Books
Cover design by Language

WHAT DOES LAW MEAN, MUMU?

A Book about the Law for Young People

Paulyn Marrinan

Porteo Marketing

To my children, Portia and Leo,
and
my angel, Guy

I dedicate this book to my grandchildren and all young people who are interested in fairness, justice and peace. I hope they will continue to probe and ask questions about legal and administrative systems to ensure that they deliver those outcomes.

Contents

One

Cultural exchange gives rise to curiosity about law – the penfriend project

It was both a happy and a sad day as we travelled to the airport. This was always a happy journey if heading off on holidays, but on that occasion Mumu was driving three young girls to drop off a very interesting young woman called Verity.

Verity always made people in her company feel happy. She had been staying with the girls for over three months on an exchange programme while she was studying to perfect her English. The three girls thought she was quite exceptional. She was very hardworking, cheerful, and generous of spirit, dedicated to improving herself on all levels, and that day she was returning home to France.

She worked as hard as she could on her studies during her English language course in Dublin, while also helping out in the family home. She even sometimes helped the girls with homework – not to mention showing them how to do French plaits in their hair. She then told everyone that she was heading back to help her parents on their farm and with the family, being the eldest of six. Verity had to go on a further work assignment before she began studying law in France in the autumn.

Mumu had asked her, for the benefit of the girls listening, how she would say that in French, to which she replied:

'Faire des etudes de droit.'

Mumu said that was an interesting use of the word for law because the word 'droit' in French also meant 'right'. As they drove along, the girls were discussing the good times they had spent with Verity and were sad that she would no longer be around.

Along the motorway Mumu saw some flashing lights ahead – a police checkpoint. She slowed down and drew up beside a police officer, who waved her down and came to the window. Everybody was very silent as the Garda peered at the paperwork on the left-hand side of the windscreen – checking the motor tax, motor insurance and car safety (NCT) certificates which, luckily, were all up to date. She then smiled, looking into the back of the car, and said, 'You have a big load in there – precious cargo – take care,' as they drove off.

Verity commented on how friendly the police officer seemed and asked what the checkpoint was about. Mumu said that maybe the checkpoint was about more serious matters, but perhaps the Guards were using the opportunity to check that motorists' paperwork was up to date.

She asked them what 'An Garda Síochána' meant. They explained that the police force in the Republic of Ireland is called 'An Garda Síochána' (which translated from the Irish language means 'the guardian of the peace'), more commonly referred to as 'the Gardaí' or simply 'the Guards'.

'I am so glad that everything was in order, otherwise I could have ended up getting a summons and paying a fine,' said Mumu. The questions then came fast and furious from the back seat.

'What is a fine? Why do we have to pay a fine?'

'If you didn't pay the fine, you would end up going to court and facing a judge if you were summoned.'

'But what is a summons? What happens if you ignore it? Couldn't you just say that you were heading off on holiday? Who makes judges? Are judges always good, Mumu?' The questions came rapidly.

'Well, girls, where should I begin?' said Mumu.

'A summons is a letter sent by a court or by some other agency or government body for various purposes. It notifies the defendant, which is the person who is being accused of something, that she or he is being told to attend court, and allows the powers of the court to hear and decide on the case. The outcome depends on the seriousness of the offence. It is a form of legal process that tells the person who is accused of doing something wrong to appear before a court on a specific day and to answer the complaint made by whoever is making that complaint. If it is a criminal matter, such as dangerous driving or causing an accident, it would be the Irish State that would 'bring the case', but if it is a non-criminal or civil matter, a case to do with some claim made by another person, the summons would be in the name of that person – called the "plaintiff" in court language. So, the official notice and summons tells the person that they have to appear in court at a certain time and in a certain place. If the accused person has to answer to a criminal charge, a Guard usually gives the person an "appearance notice" and that person would be charged with failing to appear if they did not arrive. Apart from that, it would show a great disrespect to the court. So if that person failed to turn up, the judge, who would be in charge of the court, would take a very dim view of it.

'In serious matters the judge could then issue what is described as a "Bench Warrant", in which case the Guards would go and arrest the person and bring them to court.'

'Oh, do you mean that something like stealing would be a crime, Mumu?" came a voice from behind. 'What would happen then? What happens if you steal? What's the difference between stealing and hurting somebody?'

'Oh goodness,' said Mumu. 'You have asked so many questions there and, of course, there are answers, but it would take quite a long time to give all of those answers. I think it would be interesting to know how all of these matters are dealt with in Verity's country, wouldn't it.'

Everybody remained silent and Verity smiled. Then Mumu said:

'Well, if we consider that all the law is there to protect people and to ensure that there is fairness and justice, then it would be interesting to look at the way things are done in other countries – or at least in one other country to start with, for comparison purposes – and to find out whether things are different to ours, in reaching a fair outcome. So we could consider whether there are many differences in their system of justice. Is it different from the way we do things? Is it just that we all do things differently to arrive at the same result or are the outcomes in any way different?

'After all, every country has its own traditions and policies, so for those who wish to know more about the role of legal processes in a particular nation, they really would have to go into the subject a little bit more deeply.'

Then, after a silence, Mumu said:

'I've just had a very good idea. Verity, you are about to start studying law and both you and the girls are feeling very sad about not being with each other anymore and not talking to each other every day because your lives will be so busy and there won't be time for that.'

'Oh, I know, it's okay,' came a voice from the back. 'People are going to say that we can keep in touch by Facebook or by texting.'

'Is that really keeping in touch? I would just like to tell you all about something people did in what you all would think were "the olden days", but not so long ago, when people used to write letters to each other. Without mobile phones and the internet through which to send messages, people wrote to one another. They handwrote letters, sometimes on carefully selected notepaper, if their budget permitted. Such notepaper was very often gratefully received as birthday or Christmas presents. It was good to have your favourite coloured notepaper when writing to friends or your family if you were away from them. At a time when people could not travel widely abroad, when air travel was expensive, they did not go on so many continental holidays so they really knew little about the way of life in other countries, such as details about how people lived or how things were organised. So it was very common for people to have what were called "penfriends".

'Now, here is my idea. Why not all decide that Verity will be your penfriend, as part of a special penfriend project? Studying law, she will be finding out new things about the laws in her country and, if you are interested, you can go on a journey of discovery with me to find out about some of the important aspects of the legal system in our country, and then you can write to Verity and discuss some of the discoveries that you have made and ask her about how those things differ in her country.

'You will not have to do it in handwriting; do not worry! I could imagine your protests and pleas about that. You can write to her about some of the subjects in which you are interested. Say, for example, we discuss the courts and the work of the judges and lawyers, and you find that interesting, then she can have a look at what you have found out and, as she is learning about all that in France, she can send you a summary of what she has discovered. That way, you will be able to compare the way things are done in the different systems. So you will find out about the legal system in France and she will find out about the legal systems in Ireland and common law countries.'

This idea seemed to receive great support immediately from all four, particularly from Verity, who said it would be very interesting for her to be able to have material for projects, so she could make comparisons and think about how and why things are done, as her studies progressed, by comparing the French way to the way things were done elsewhere.

The conversation was getting more serious now, and as they could see the airport drawing closer they were feeling a little sad about saying the final 'goodbye' to Verity, so Mumu decided to try to cheer them up a little bit by remembering some interesting ideas put to her recently by a witty colleague. The girls had heard this story already so, hearing it for the second time, they knew exactly what the outcome was going to be.

Mumu began to recall what this person had written to her.

'For people like me who do not and cannot relate to Facebook and communicate personal matters "publicly", I have been trying to make friends outside of Facebook while applying the same principles.

'Therefore, every day I walk down the street and tell passers-by what I have eaten, how I feel at the moment, what I have done the night before, what I will do later and with whom. I give them pictures of my family, my dog, and of me gardening, taking things apart in the garage, watering the lawn, standing in front of landmarks, driving around town, having lunch and doing what anybody and everybody does every day. I also listen to their conversations, give them a "thumbs up" and tell them I "like" them, and it works, just like Facebook. The news is I already have four people following me: two Guards, a private investigator, and a psychiatrist.'

Verity laughed heartily at this story as they approached the drop-off point at the airport.

Mumu pulled in, put on the flashing lights, and everybody got out on the safe side to help Verity take out her suitcases, help her put them on the trolley and give her farewell hugs. They told her how much they appreciated all she had done for them, while looking somewhat sad, and quickly Verity responded:

'But this is not the end of our relationship. From what we have been discussing, this is now the beginning of a new penfriend project, which will be a journey of learning and discovering how the law works in different countries.

'I am really looking forward to this discussion between us. This will be so educational and interesting'.

As Mumu stood back watching this exchange, she thought to herself that this was very typical of Verity, who was the essence of what everybody would consider to be a bright young person with a very honest outlook on life and an interest in people. Unsurprising, she thought to herself. Some day this girl will make a very good lawyer.

They waited until she went into the departure area, where she joined her friends, with whom she was returning to France. They could see her through the doors going to the check-in desks and then Mumu gradually drove off as the group gave those final waves that we are never sure have been seen or not by the other person.

Two

The journey towards the penfriend project – crimes – presumption of innocence – evidence – police forces – support from the people

Knowing that everybody was feeling a little downhearted, Mumu said nothing for a while, but this silence was very quickly broken by the enthusiastic voice of the girl who had moved into the front – the eldest of the three, who were called Nova, Aver and Preuve.

'I think that's a very good idea, Mumu – the penfriend project. I feel so excited about it,' said Nova.

Preuve and Aver, from the back seat, exclaimed together: 'Yes, it's a great idea and we could all do it together – all contribute.'

Nova continued, 'Now that it's in my head, Mumu, I have lots of questions coming; what about the police, what happens if there are "baddy policemen"? What does it mean to be arrested? What's the difference between a crime against a person and a crime against property? What is the difference between all the courts? And a parking fine – what is it, why do we have to pay fines? Why do we have to go to court?

'Oh, I have so many questions. What are the rules? Who makes the rules? Who makes judges? Are judges always good?'

'Well,' said Mumu, 'you have asked a number of questions there and I have an idea. Before school opens, maybe we should go into the courts and look at what goes on and see where the story, in some senses, begins. Let us go and get a feeling of the surroundings where the daily practice of the law takes place. Of course, there are courts in all the other towns and cities but, for this project, we will just focus on the one that is the nearest to us, in Dublin.

'So, for the moment, to "get the ball rolling", let me give you a few brief answers to some of the questions you asked. You can all sit back and just listen to what I am saying and then, perhaps, when we have our visit to the courts, you can ask more detailed questions. You asked me about a parking fine. We could start by saying that we have rules in so many situations, and we accept that we need rules. You asked me who makes the rules. What is the idea of the rules? The rules of public order and conduct are looked after by the Guards, but those rules about parking – who makes those up?

'Well,' said Mumu, addressing her list of their questions. 'We all live under rules of some kind; we put our dirty dishes away, we make our beds, we keep our school books clean and obey the school rules. We know that if we are playing a game, or any sport, there will be a referee who will blow the whistle to signal: "No, you are out of order: you've broken the rules". So, if we were designing an imaginary game or world, first of all there has to be a plan about the aims and goals and then discussions and consensus on the necessary rules to achieve those goals.

'The next stage would be to make the rules known to people – to promulgate them. That is a great word, isn't it? It means to spread the news far and wide to all who will be affected by the rules. So then, when we all understand the rules, we need to agree who is the referee in charge of maintaining these rules, and respect their authority. This individual or authority needs to be in a position to tell us when we have broken the rules and punish those who break them. In soccer that might be a yellow or red card, and if it is in relation to motoring laws it might be a fine, penalty points on the driver's licence, or more severe penalties, depending on how serious the breaches of the rules are. That authority or referee accepts the power given by us to keep control. We have to keep the rules, but maybe, sometimes, we might look at the rules and say, "Well, are all these rules any good? Maybe some of them could be updated?"

'But for the purposes of your notebook, which you are going to get to start this project, you might like to write down any rules in your school that you think are not so effective and would benefit from a review that might make things better for everyone.'

A question came from Aver at the back:

'But if the legal system is different in every country, Mumu, which is better?'

'No, we can't talk about one being better than the other. Different countries have different cultures, different ways of doing things, different laws, different beliefs, different ways of organising the way they live. We have to respect that there are ways that are not the same as ours. But, I agree, from what we said earlier, it would be good to find out, by comparing our ways in general to one other country, as in this penfriend project. We could first see whether they are aiming for the same results but just doing it differently, or whether, in doing it differently, the results are very different.'

'Remember, Mumu, when we were talking the other day about everybody being innocent until they were proved guilty and you told us that that was called "a presumption of innocence"?' said Aver. 'I have forgotten why you said that was so valuable.'

'Well, that is a great question. What would you think if a person who was accused of doing something bad was put in prison because they could not prove their innocence? For example, if they were to be punished because they were wrongly identified? If they were not the person who stole the wallet or they were not the person who broke into the house? Say, for example, a Guard had come along and had seen a dark shadow running along the laneway beside a house that had been burgled, and chased that person, but that was not the person who had broken into the house. So, it is a very important right for citizens that we believe that an accused person is innocent until the State (that is, really, the country acting on behalf of all the citizens) can produce enough evidence to prove that this was the person who had broken in. That might be as a result of matching the person's fingerprints to ones that were on the door handles or on surfaces in the house.

'It might be bringing in three or four reliable witnesses who could say, "I saw that person. The lighting was good. I saw them going up to that front door taking out a screwdriver and breaking in."

'Maybe another person might say, "I saw them breaking in and then I hid behind a hedge and I phoned the Guards on my mobile phone and I saw them coming out again and they were carrying a bag that looked as if it was bulging with things. I saw an Xbox sticking out of the top."

'Maybe a third person could say, "I saw them jumping into a car where a driver was waiting and they drove away at high speed."

'Only when the court and the jury, if there is one, is satisfied that there is enough evidence "beyond a reasonable doubt" is the person found guilty. "Beyond a reasonable doubt" means that there must be 100 per cent certainty on the part of the jurors (the members of the jury) when they are arriving at that decision. If there is the slightest doubt in their minds about the evidence against the accused person, then they have to find them "not guilty". Can you understand why we have to be so careful?'

'Well, it is very serious if you are going to find somebody guilty of a crime, because that may mean them going to prison. That means that they are going to lose their freedom for the length of time that they are sent away,' said Nova.

'Yes,' said Mumu, 'it would change their lives forever, because if you go to prison you then have what is called "a criminal record", which means that if, for example, you look for a job, possible employers would see that you had been in prison. Then there might be serious doubts about whether they would give that person a job and, in fact, it is the case that people who have been in prison, even though they may have sought forgiveness, changed their ways, undergone training and further education in prison, still find it difficult to get a job. This is one way that the "cycle of crime" begins. Some people call it the "revolving door" because those people will lose the hope of a normal way of life and their self-respect will be low, so there are greater risks of them associating with people still involved in criminal activity and the chances of them getting caught up in that way of life are increased, so they can find themselves "behind bars" again.

'So, it is a very serious step to find somebody guilty and send them to prison. Therefore, the courts have to be very careful that if somebody is to be found guilty they are sure that it is the right person. We are very lucky in Ireland to have what we describe as the "presumption of innocence".'

'I understand what you mean, Mumu,' said Preuve, 'but is the jury or the court always right in their decision?'

'It is possibly the time to mention that there have been cases, within our legal systems and others, where people were sent to prison who were innocent and who, for many years, tried to make their case of innocence from prison. Supporters, like their lawyers, members of their family, or a particular journalist, might have campaigned fervently on their behalf. They might have had to protest the innocence of the person for years, seeking a retrial by coming up with further evidence to suggest that the finding of the court was wrong. Sometimes it has happened that, after a case has been reviewed and errors found in the evidence that was used to convict the person, the person was released from prison.'

'Oh no,' said Aver, 'that is awful. What happens then?'

'Then the State has to pay them compensation for having taken away their freedom for that length of time. Such a dreadful event is called "a miscarriage of justice". Of course, this is a very serious thing because it means that the justice system has failed. And that is a very dark day for any country's legal system.'

'It must be very difficult for a person to survive something like that,' said Preuve sadly.

'Yes. But there is difference in what we call the "standards of proof" that are required in civil, rather than criminal cases. When people are contesting something in a civil court, that is called a civil dispute because it is not a criminal case. For example, someone might be claiming that the person who sold them a car knew that the car had been in an accident that had weakened its whole frame. The question is whether the seller knew or ought to have known about the previous serious damage. Where someone is defending a civil claim then the standards of proof – that means the kinds of proofs that are needed – are slightly less, and we call that "proof on the balance of probability". A good way to look at it is to imagine an old-fashioned weighing scales where two pans are balanced against each other. You are looking at all of the evidence and considering whether, for example, the argument of a person who is claiming that his neighbour trespassed onto his garden is enough to tilt the scales in one direction and persuade you what they said was actually true. I give that to you as a small example because, sadly, so many disputes arise between neighbours. We might talk about that in some detail later.

'So, girls, I'm really looking forward to your penfriend project – this discussion between you and Verity, which I hope will keep your friendship going for many years and will also prove very useful and interesting for all of you.'

They were nearly home when Mumu decided to take up one of the subjects that they had mentioned, and that was in connection with the police forces.

'You asked me about police forces. Well it is important to mention that, of course, police forces are highly trained in most countries. There are usually two kinds of police (although in some countries, like France, I believe there are more). Generally there are the uniformed police officers and the detectives, who are plain-clothes officers who do not wear a uniform. The detectives are normally sent on special assignments and play a very vital role when they are under cover, where they are not recognised as the police, so they can conduct their investigations without warning or giving a signal to the criminals that they are "on their tail".'

'We know that from films and books,' said Preuve.

'I was just thinking, girls, that it might be a very good

idea if you asked yourselves some basic questions, as you are starting on this project, such as why do most people obey most laws? Do they do it because it is the right thing to do, and they know that if everybody does it then it will keep normal social standards, maintain community spirit, and protect them and their families in the end? Or do they do it because they are afraid of being punished if they are caught?

'It is also important to say that a police force like the Gardaí, a group of people with quite substantial powers, must have legal authority to use that power. It is important to bear in mind that the police only use that power because the people – the citizens of the country – give it to them. It is an agreed relationship in a free and ordered society.

'If citizens trust the authority that is given to protect their community, then the relationship is productive, but it is a very slim, thin line that could be crossed easily if people lost trust in the use of that authority.

'Look around and see how a police force wins or loses that vital trust. It is often said that in a democracy – a free society like Ireland, where people have an opportunity of voting for a government at regular intervals, with open and fair elections – the police force only exists through a relationship of respect and support from their community.

'You asked me earlier whether there were "baddy policemen". Well, of course, unfortunately, sometimes there are, as there are in any large groups of people who have certain powers. There is an odd expression that covers that. Often people say that "in a barrel of fresh apples there is always one that will be rotten at the bottom of the barrel." So, unfortunately, sometimes the rot sets in and maybe somebody does something less than good in the force, or in the group. That can influence others to follow and sometimes there are bad practices that creep in, but they are usually discovered and, when this happens, corrective actions are taken.'

Nova looked worried. 'What happens to a baddy police officer?'

'If the officer had been accused of doing something illegal, they would be prosecuted, or brought to court to answer charges. If what they did was a breach of their own rules of conduct, then action would be taken through their disciplinary procedures, which are very strict.

'First of all, the charges against the police officer would be examined inside the force and then they would go before a panel for a "disciplinary hearing". If the panel hearing that case found them to be in breach of a particular code of conduct, then the officer would have an opportunity of appealing that decision through a second layer of protection, as it were, to make sure that the disciplinary procedure was balanced and fair. So they would then have a right to pass on the finding of the board to a disciplinary appeals tribunal.

'There are senior people who sit on that tribunal. It is chaired by a judge or senior counsel barrister, and there will be somebody representing the Garda commissioner, the head of the police force here, and somebody from the body of which the police officer is a member – either the Association of Garda Sergeants and Inspectors (AGSI) or the Garda Representative Association (GRA). They test and examine the evidence all over again, and the police officer has a chance to go through what their defence was and point out why they believe that the original disciplinary hearing was mistaken in its findings.'

The group had been listening very attentively. Preuve asked if the people could put trust in the police force. Mumu thought before answering, and said:

'I think in spite of the many exceptions and people who brought the force into a bad light at times, we are very lucky here that we have a good police force and one we can trust.

'Let me tell you a story. One evening, a while back, there was a series of international music festivals down by the seafront in Dublin, where there was a large grassy area big enough for bands and the audience. I walked along to where there was a band playing. There were crowds gathered of young and not so young people, all expecting a good evening of music.

'I stopped where there was a good view, to the left of the stage, and stood on the edge of the crowd, just listening to the music and watching the reactions of the audience, who seemed to be enjoying it thoroughly. I noticed that from three sides of this semi-circular shape around the stage, three sets of two members of the Guards approached slowly and stood on the edge of the gathering. Two of them happened to be female officers and the other two pairs were male. As they came to a stop to the rear of the audience, the lead singer, who was holding the microphone, stopped singing abruptly and said very loudly and very aggressively, "Oh here come the rats", and with that there was a silent pause, followed by what I would describe as a sort of groaning silence from what had been a highly excited audience up until that point. They had been swaying and moving to the music. But now the silence became darker and darker, and then all of the audience together started a slow handclap. Do you know what that means?'

'No, Mumu, we don't know what that means,' they all answered together, so engrossed were they in the story.

'Well, if you give a slow handclap to somebody who is performing, it is a sign that you do not approve. To get the message across you very slowly and very thoughtfully clap your hands, as if to say: "No, no, this is not good enough; we don't like what we are hearing."

'This came across as a united message, the band members looked confused, and then the slow rhythmic signal was interrupted by somebody shouting: "Give it up for the Guards!" At that point all the audience started to clap approvingly and let out a cheer.

'I thought that was very interesting. I went for the rest of my walk and later, as I was returning to where my car was parked, I saw the two female Guards walking in my direction. I recognised one because, coincidentally, she had taken part in a postgraduate course that I had run in Trinity College a couple of years back called *Conflict and Dispute Resolution Studies.*

'As we drew closer, she recognised me. I greeted her and asked her how she was getting on. We exchanged information and updates on some of the other people on the course from her year and she explained that she had kept in touch with some of them, as she introduced me to her colleague.

'Then I mentioned what I had seen and she said that that was not unusual. They had noticed on many other occasions that when they were "policing" a crowd – keeping a steady but discreet watch over a large event like that, to protect people just in case there was any kind of trouble, and to see if there was any bad behaviour such as the passing of drugs or the drinking of alcohol in public, both of which would be prohibited by the law – the members of the crowd appreciated their presence. It was encouraging to see that people in a group like that had used their judgement and given their answer, and were not going to allow somebody to come and describe members of their police force as "rats" and belittle their duty in protecting people, upholding the law and guarding the peace.'

As they drew nearer their house, Mumu thought that the group would be rather tired, but they were still eager to agree on a plan, which was that they would all get very large notebooks dedicated to the penfriend project and they would start writing about their experiences and asking questions arising from the rather hurried discussion they had already had.

They looked forward to visiting the courts to have a look around and "start at the centre", as it were, of where the action takes place in the court and judicial system.

'Thank you very much, Mumu,' said Aver as she closed the car door.

Three

Mumu talks to her band of learners about the law and democracy

As Mumu was approaching the Four Courts she spoke to the group. Nova and Aver had asked if they could bring along two cousins, Rex and Lex, as Preuve had gone to her friend's house.

'You asked me a number of questions, like "Who is in charge?", "Who appoints judges?", "Who is in charge of the police?' and "Where do the rules come from?"

'So I think we should start by talking about the way we organise our country. I will try not to use too many very big words, but I realise also that you have read so many novels and wonderful books that have very complicated themes, not to mention very complicated characters, with very complex vocabulary.

'The word "democracy" describes the system by which we run the business of our country. In a democracy the aim is to involve all of the people in the formation of policies that will reflect how the majority want things done. The theory is that the whole population, or all of the people who are eligible to vote, should have a say in how things are done through exercising their franchise, which is that precious right to cast a vote through elected representatives – at local government and at central government level when there is a general election.'

'What is "local government", Mumu?' asked Aver.

'We have local councils of elected representatives who have a role in organising some aspects of our services in their areas, or zones, of the cities and counties where the areas are divided up. During local elections, we have a chance to vote for a local councillor, who may be an independent or a member of a political party. Then we have the right to vote for a representative – a member of parliament, called a TD in Ireland – through general elections.

'Before an election the political parties draw up a manifesto, which is a detailed plan, with costings, of their policies, in which they are supposed to set out clearly how they hope to pay for all the social and other services provided for citizens without raising the taxes so high that the voters will reject them. Then the parties campaign; they put up posters and their supporters call to people's doors, which is called "canvassing", trying to win trust and encourage voters to give them their vote. There may also be people who run for office as independents, which means that they stand for some causes but are not in any of the main political parties. The party that wins most votes, and gains a majority, forms the government. All the people who voted for them give them the authority to deliver on the promises they made in their manifesto. This is called a mandate. If there is no clear majority then the largest party will have to negotiate with the next largest group, and even independents, to make up what is described as a working majority. This is called a coalition government.

'The parliament does not just have the members who form the government sitting in it. It has all of the other representatives who "won a seat", as we call it, doing the very important job of forming the opposition in that parliament, making sure that the government is held to account and that it works according the promises that it made to the electorate when it was trying to win the election. You have probably seen television debates from the House of Commons in the UK or our parliament here, the Dail, where the parties are quite vigorously calling the other side to account and questioning the ministers responsible for various pieces of legislation as to how this is going to go through, or criticising them for failures in the health, education, housing or other essential services.'

'Mumu, excuse me, but do they discuss new laws? And how do you get into parliament? I mean, can anybody be a member of parliament?' asked Lex.

'Yes, all of the members of parliament can debate and test the details of proposed legislation, which is called a "bill" at that stage. It might be a bill proposed by the minister for health or the minister for justice. It might be what is called a "private member's bill", which a member can bring to parliament for discussion. In many countries, as in Ireland, France and the UK, to name a few, there is what we call an upper chamber. In Ireland we call it the Senate and in the UK it is known as the House of Lords. It is where you have another layer of people who can discuss proposed legislation and debate it before it is "signed into law" by the head of state. They have a little bit more time to do that in more detail than the working members of parliament, who are out working on constituency matters and seeing to their duties every day.

'So the members of the upper chamber, or the upper house, can spend a little bit more time researching and examining the legislation that is going through in draft stages for their review. Some senates or upper chambers have people who are elected and some have a system of appointment to that upper layer of parliament. I hope that this makes some sense. I do not want to go into too much detail on every subject because we can return to these matters later if you want to. Is that alright?'

'Yes,' replied Nova, 'that makes sense, because we need to learn the basic facts before we start to list the main topics for our letters to Verity.'

'Does everyone agree with that?'

Agreement was reached by all in the rear of the car and Lex seemed to have understood.

'You have an interesting name, Lex, which is particularly suited to our discussion. Do you know what your name means?'

'Yes,' replied Lex. 'My teacher said that when I went to school, and she wanted to know if my parents had told me the meaning. She said that Lex is the Latin word for "law" or "statute". My parents were impressed when I told them that and said that they thought I would be too young to understand that at the time; but I did understand!'

Nova laughed, and Aver asked about Latin, but Mumu said that Latin was an old language which was 'the root' of many modern languages.

'It is used in science, botany, medicine, pharmacy, music and the law, and we might discuss that a bit later.

'Before talking about Latin, it might be more helpful if we stay on the topics we have been discussing today, so I hope you will be patient, Aver. There are many Latin expressions used in law and we shall return to that subject.'

'Okay, Mumu.'

'I used the word "legislation" just now and that brings

us to another basic part of our democratic system, which is called the "separation of powers". This is extremely important, because it is one of the foundations of a truly working democracy. It means that the legislators – the people who bring in the laws, on our behalf, in the parliament are separate from the judiciary – the judges, who are independent in exercising their function – who, in turn, are separate from the executive or government running the country at any particular time.

'So, "separation of powers" is really a constitutional principle that limits the powers of any person or institution. It divides the governmental authority into three branches: the legislative which is the parliament or the senate or both; the executive, which is the prime minister and her or his government; and the judiciary, which is headed up by the chief justice, who is the top judge, and other judges. We would call this a "political doctrine" or "constitutional protection" under which the three branches of the government (executive, legislative and judicial) are kept separate to prevent any abuse of power. It is also known as a system of "checks and balances" whereby every branch is given certain powers protected in its function, but with the other branches to keep it under review and accountable.

'I hope this answers some of the questions that you asked me earlier about the courts and the judges and the parliament?'

Nova smiled, looking around at the others, and said that they had all discussed this adventure after their last outing and that they thought that some of the information about legal systems might be difficult to understand. They agreed that they would put down questions in their notebooks if something needed to be explained later.

'Well, I am very impressed by that,' replied Mumu.

'You also asked me how people get into parliament, and

someone asked if anybody can be a member of parliament. The correct answer to that is that not everybody can be but, in theory, everybody has the freedom to put themselves forward, and I suppose that is really the underlying difference and value of an open and free democracy. You can "run for parliament" – that is, put yourself forward – when there is a general election or a local election by registering as a candidate. You can put out your placards to show what you represent and try to persuade and encourage people to vote for you. You have to put down a deposit of money, which is a good idea to give some level of control over the numbers of people wanting to put themselves forward. However, it does not stop quite extreme people sometimes running as candidates and having a go. It is sometimes said jokingly that the UK and Ireland have always been a bit of a breeding ground for eccentrics and, as an example of this, we can look to a time in the 1970s and later, when there was a young man who used to call himself Screaming Lord Sutch, who put himself forward as a candidate at the time of elections in London. He was probably the ultimate example of this. He was the leader and founder of many small so-called "political parties". One of his better-known ones was called The Monster Raving Loony Party. He stood for forty-nine elections and earned a place in the *Guinness Book of Records*. However, he "lost his deposit", as they say. That means that he forfeited the amount of money he put forward as a deposit to allow him to run on all of those occasions. He was, of course, a colourful character with his trademark gold lamé top hat and leopard skin jacket festooned with rosettes and badges.

'And of course, more recently, we had a "Lord Buckethead" in the elections in the UK. We could, on one hand, say that it is proof of a free and open democracy that people can put themselves forward. On the other hand, you could say that such a person was showing a dislike of the system and flaunting himself as a rebel. But, without really having very much to back up what he was standing for, other than just opposing what is in place, perhaps it was just about his own personal vanity and an attempt to be a celebrity. The question remains open, and we can ask whether there was a value in such a person showing that elections were open and available for anyone who thought that they had some reason for putting themselves forward as a likely representative of certain people and their views and interests. But we must be wary because some people might represent very extreme and dangerous views that could threaten the stability and safety of our society.

'Freedom of speech is one of the foundations of a free and open society, but there is a thin line over which people can stray to put forward dangerous threats against others. So we have laws to protect against what we describe as "hate speech" or "incitement to violence".'

'Did Screaming Lord Sutch have many supporters?' asked Nova.

'I would say that, if he did, they were also showing dislike of the system,' suggested Rex, and then asked whether governments always kept their promises.

'I think a handful of supporters answers that, Nova. Yes, dislike is a good word, Rex. Also, we must bear in mind that there have been people described as "anarchists" down through the ages. They are usually opposed to the social systems and the established order and set out to undermine the benefit of the prevailing systems. Generally speaking, they believe in the abolition of all governments and the organisation of society on a voluntary, co-operative basis without having force or compulsion, but I must be careful not to generalise on this topic. However, they do not recognise authority and aim to discredit that. Then there are "nihilists", who appear to believe there is no purpose or value in anything – being pessimistic people who see no meaning or merit in common values. But again this is a very deep topic and requires further analysis and commentary.

'You might all introduce these subjects at school when the teacher introduces times for discussions. It would be interesting to hear all the different views and interpretations of these topics.'

'Mumu, I am trying to follow all of that and some of it makes sense to me,' said Nova.

'Please do not worry, we can go over some of the more difficult ideas another time or, if you put some of the subjects up for discussion with your teachers, you will learn more.

'One of you asked me earlier whether the people really decided on everything about running their country and, in many ways, it is hard to answer this question because you could meet many people who would say they feel that they do not "have a voice", that they are not properly represented, and they feel that perhaps sometimes politicians are "at one step removed" from the realities of everyday life. It can be frustrating for people who experience this and who try to find a way of influencing politics at a local and, ultimately, at a central level so that their needs, the needs of their families, are properly addressed and recognised.

'And this leads me to the other question that you asked me earlier about what happens if the government fails to run the country properly. This is where the checks and balances that we referred to earlier apply. If the government fails to run the country properly then the opposition, which should be working hard to call the government to task, will reveal any of the mistakes that it makes and will expose any of its wrongdoing to the public – who can judge for themselves how effectively they have performed. Then, when it comes to a general election, they may not give that party a vote.

'Normally general elections are held every four or so years, depending on the country in question. The people also have another way of expressing their dissatisfaction. If, for example, a member of parliament dies, there has to be an election in the area which he represented – a by-election, as it is called. The government party candidate might not win a majority of the votes so the government's majority could slip a little, in which case it would be edging nearer and nearer to having to call a general election. This is called "going back to the people again". Also, if the government is not fulfilling its mandate by working through the manifesto, which is what it said it would do when it was asking for people to give it support as a political party running for office, then it might notice a reduction in its support through opinion polls, which are conducted regularly. Have you heard of them?'

'Oh yes,' came the reply from the group.

'We heard about those on the news,' said Rex.

'The opposition party might apply pressure for an election by intensive debates and criticism in parliament, which might result in a "vote of no confidence" in the prime minister to undermine the stability of the party in power and cause an election to let the people decide. The results might provide a victory for the biggest party in opposition, and that would be proof that faith in the government had become less.

'So, the government has to be held to task, and if it is not doing its job properly it should suffer the consequences by having to go back to the people again for reaffirmation of the majority's confidence in it to do its work. As we have already mentioned, if one party does not have a workable majority, it might have to negotiate with other parties to form a coalition government to work together in the interests of the common good of the country.'

'That is so much information. I never knew that there was so much going on and that it was so complicated. I can understand how people might be frustrated if the government did not keep its promises,' said Aver.

'Yes; that is why I said that all of this should raise your awareness, your curiosity to find out more through discussions within school and college.

'Someone asked me who was allowed to vote – or does everybody have a vote? What is so special about having a vote and do all people all over the world have a vote? Did women always have the vote?

'First of all, in a proper functioning democracy everybody over the age of 18 (if that is the legal age) should be allowed to vote. Does that happen in every country in the world? Sadly, the answer is no, but that's what we are all working towards. When you ask what is so special about having a vote, I think the best way I can answer that question is to ask you to look at television news coverage of countries where people have not had a vote until recently or where there have not been "free elections", with a ruler staying in power for many years and not having fair elections, which means that the people may have been frightened and oppressed so the elections were not a true reflection of their views.

'I would ask you to look at the queues of people in countries like Zimbabwe, where they recently had a change of leadership; and watch people queuing in their hundreds, from early morning, outside the polling stations – queuing up to exercise their right as a citizen to have a say in the outcome of the election for a new government or president. I think this should answer your question. The countries where people have had to struggle to have a vote, to fight for that independence, to fight for that right, show

how precious and important the right to vote is. It will be interesting to read what Verity has to say about all this.

'For example, in the Republic of South Africa, having the vote for all black people was so important to change things in that country. It was not until 1994 that "universal suffrage" was introduced. I am sure that you have heard of the famous campaigner who became leader of that country, Nelson Mandela, who took on the struggle for democracy over many years – many of which he spent in prison. Suffrage is a good word to think about; it has its roots in Latin and French, so Verity will know about this too.

'As for the other question, did women always have a vote? Of course, the answer is no. I think some of you have learned about the Suffragettes and the long, bitter fight for the vote for women, because we were recently celebrating one hundred years of the breakthrough of women getting the vote both here in Ireland and in the UK, so you may know a little bit about the struggle of the Suffragettes and the women who fought for that right, and the risk to which they put their own lives during that struggle.

'After that hard-won fight, from 1918 women in Ireland and the United Kingdom could vote, but it was a "qualified right" because they could only vote at the age of thirty with certain property requirements or in university constituencies, while men could vote at the age of twenty-one with no qualifications. When Ireland gained its full independence in 1922, the Irish Free State gave equal voting rights to men and to women and, eventually, in the United Kingdom the franchise was extended similarly to women in 1928.'

'Why are votes so important, Mumu?' asked Aver.

Then Nova interrupted and said: 'Oh, Aver, please catch up; how could you ask such a question at this stage!'

'Let us find a way of explaining, Nova. We must not be impatient. Aver, from what we have said so far, why do you think having a vote is so important? Let us look at it the other way round: what is the opposite of that? If democracy means that it is a free and open society and that all of the eligible people are allowed to vote – those over 18 years of age who can exercise a choice about how they want their country run and in whose hands they are prepared to trust the running of that country. If people do not have that, what is the alternative? Possibly someone taking power by force, or one who takes power slyly through a vote but then discards the laws providing the voting protections and runs the country as a tyrant.

'Can you imagine that, and how life would be where there is no opportunity to object or to criticise or to have confidence or faith that there is going to be open and fair organisation of the country for the appointment of independent judges and a police force? Imagine no transparent controls of the police, defence forces and all the heads of the organisations running a country. Can you just imagine the threat that there would be to people without confidence in the running of their police force or the independence of their justice system? Just imagine the scene that I have told you about before at the music festival and the band having an automatic response to the members of the police force who came down to quietly and effectively monitor and protect the people gathered there in a large crowd. If that had been in a country where there was no democracy, then you can imagine if they had said, "Here comes the rats," what the retaliation would have been and how they would have been treated for having spoken out against the police.'

Then, as if to defend herself for not being able to keep up, Aver added: 'Well, there seems to be different systems in different countries, so then do we have to say that some are better than others?'

'Well, Aver, we do not want to become very proud

of what we have but at the same time criticise other countries when perhaps those people are struggling for reforms. We might know that they have limited rights but we have to be discreet, because we do not want to offend other people. It is difficult to believe that people would voluntarily accept government systems in which they appear to have little control or any say in how things are run.

'It is worth mentioning the system of a people's vote. We have often made use of the referendum process, in this country, when big decisions have to be made after reforming or changing laws; in summary, this involves putting the relevant question in a way that requires a "yes" or "no" vote by all the people. We had Marriage Equality and Termination of Pregnancy referendum processes recently. In 2016, in the UK, they used the referendum model to vote on whether or not to leave the European Union. But now we see that arguably a "yes" or "no" vote was not sufficient to provide the people with all the information they needed to understand the many implications of leaving the European Union – that it was not just a simple single step without political and other consequences. The people voting "yes" did so by a small majority, but a majority nonetheless. However, in light of the many complications arising from such a move by the United Kingdom, there were even calls, by some, for a second referendum in which some of the controversial or complex implications could be clarified, so that the people's vote would be informed and not a decision made without people being aware of consequential problems arising for the country and its responsibilities; for example, to the Belfast Agreement, which was negotiated after a delicately managed peace process in Northern Ireland, to which the British government was a signatory.'

Four

A visit to the courts – Lady Justice – wigs and gowns – the snail in the ginger beer – women and the law

'So today we are off to the courts. It is interesting to see the way the word "court" is used. We talk about "going to court", maybe to seek our rights in an action or a case, as it known, if we have a claim against someone. Matters are said to be "referred to the courts". We talk of the "courts of justice". We could say that they are the stages on which the legal systems are played out, with all the players performing their parts, whether it is a criminal matter or a civil claim. The courts themselves, these "theatres of justice", are divided into layers; there are District Courts in local areas and the Circuit Courts in main towns and cities, where cases up to a certain monetary limit are heard. And then there are the High Courts, the Courts of Appeal and, ultimately, the highest court – the Supreme Court, which is over all of these courts. Today we will visit the area known as the Four Courts, Ireland's main courts building, recognisable along the banks of the River Liffey in Dublin by the large dome under which all of the courts are to be found, centred around a large hall. Dotted around these High Courts there are other Circuit Courts and District Courts and Family Courts and Children's Courts in the immediate area.'

Mumu parked the car and led the group of four, two girls and two boys, all carrying their notebooks, towards the outside of the Four Courts. Before they arrived at the main entrance, she stopped for a moment to discuss something interesting.

'Well, we are now going to enter this huge building, with lots of other buildings in the adjoining streets, but let us look just at the design and the character of this world, which has its own formalities. We must remember the history that made it as it is. Let us think about "the symbols of justice". How many times have you seen the statue of a large female figure, either standing or sitting, holding a weighing scales in one hand and in her other hand holding a sword – and sometimes she is blindfolded? You will see this image repeated in many textbooks. Those imposing statues outside courts are known as Lady Justice. She is a powerful symbol as she sits outside the Central Criminal Court in London, in Belfast or other courts. What do you think is the meaning of Lady Justice? What do you think of the symbols?'

There was silence and nobody came up with an idea.

'It is a hard question. Well, let us look at the Scales of Justice – that balance she holds in one hand. Tell me what you think that means.'

Lex was very excited to offer his suggestion that this was weighing up the balance of the evidence to see which way it tilted; and that was a perfect answer.

'And the sword?'

'Well,' said Lex, 'could that be about punishment?'

'Well done,' said Mumu, 'that's perfectly correct, yes.

If the person was not innocent they were going to be punished in some way. If it was a serious criminal case or if it was a civil case, it might mean that they would lose whatever it was they were claiming was their right and they might have to pay the costs of having taken the case in the first place.

'And what about the blindfold part?'

Rex came up with a good suggestion.

'Would that mean that it was justice without recognising the people or favouring one person over the other?'

Mumu replied, 'Well done, you are all very interested in this. Yes, it was really to show that the identity, or the status and the wealth of the person, would not affect the outcome of the case – that everybody would be treated equally before the law. Lady Justice was viewed more as an artistic symbol than an actual deity, with religious significance, but the image has lasted and you might be surprised to find these symbols outside courthouses in far-flung countries. We are all very familiar with the television news broadcasts covering a controversial case. For example, whenever the television news teams go to the courts in London, especially the famous court known as the Old Bailey, the camera might focus on the beautiful statue of Lady Justice, in which she has no blindfold, but with her sword and her scales she is there to remind everybody that this is where hopefully people get justice and fairness.

'I was interested to see that even in countries like Brazil, which have some new modern court buildings, they have adorned those buildings with sculptures depicting Lady Justice in a modern art style.

'In ancient times, it is said that emperors had statues of Lady Justice in their palaces to give the impression of how good they were. Is it fair to see male rulers using the

Lady Justice symbol to gain respect when they would not give women equal rights and protections and respect in their countries?

'Can you think of a word for that?'

Nova said, 'Hypocrisy comes to mind.'

'Yes, Nova. I think hypocrisy will do for the moment, thank you.

'Many people have had to fight for the right of access to justice over many years to make sure that the system in their countries was fair. But many say that if you have rights, you also have responsibilities, so you have to be a good citizen and respect the laws in your country and respect the rights of others. What do you think is good about that? Does that sound sensible to you? What are your thoughts about all of that? Let's put those down as questions to discuss later. Perhaps this is something you could bring up in a discussion at school when you are having an open time for debate about current affairs or matters of interest and, indeed, it would be very interesting to bring that up in your penfriend project with Verity.

'Without getting too serious about it, I would suggest that you could summarise all of that by the simple expression: "Do unto others as they would do unto you." The best test is to ask how you expect people to treat you. Do you agree? If you hope to be treated fairly and respected by people, you have to treat them fairly and with respect also. True or false?'

'I think that is hard to think about every day,' said Rex.

'But surely, that is quite obvious?' said Lex.

'We are always taught to treat those around us in the way we would hope to be treated,' said Nova.

'Yes, we have that printed in a frame on the wall of our classroom,' said Aver.

'Let me try to bring alive some examples for you where people have "made the law". We shall get to this subject in a bit more detail when we start to look at the difference between the law in this part of the world, which is known as the common law, and the kind of system of law which operates in France, where Verity lives. Countries like France and other continental European nations have what is known as civil law, which is generally traced back to the code of laws compiled by the Roman Emperor Justinian around AD 600. Laws were then developed, over many centuries in various countries, leading to similar legal systems, all with their own sets of rules and laws. By comparison, common law evolved over time by agreement and precedent – and I'll explain what I mean by precedent when we talk a bit more about that.

'So civil law systems are systems which are more generally based on a written code of law. Without revealing anything that Verity is going to tell you, French law has *droit privé* and *droit public,* and these are part of what is known as the Civil Code, which means that they have a written civil law – administrative law going back to the old Napoleonic Code where there was a Civil Code and a Fiscal Code and a Penal Code.

'As Verity will tell you, the roles of lawyer and judge are different in each system. In civil law countries judges are often described as "investigators". They generally take the lead in the proceedings by bringing charges, establishing fact through witness examination, and applying remedies found in the legal codes. Lawyers still represent the interests of their clients in civil proceedings but have less of a central role. As in common law systems, their tasks commonly include advising clients on points of law and preparing legal pleadings for filing with the court. But the importance of oral argument, in court presentations and active lawyering in court, is less when compared to common law systems. In addition, non-litigation legal tasks, such as the preparation of a will or the drafting of a contract, may be left to a quasi-legal professional – that is, someone who is not fully qualified – who serves business and private individuals, and who may not have a post-university legal education or be licensed to practise before the courts. In contrast, in common law countries lawyers make presentations to the judge (and sometimes to a jury) and examine witnesses themselves. The proceedings are then, if you like, "refereed" by the judge, who has somewhat greater flexibility than in a civil law system to fashion or moderate an appropriate remedy at the conclusion of the case. In these cases, lawyers stand before the court and attempt to persuade the court on points of law and fact, and maintain a very active role in legal proceedings. And unlike certain civil law jurisdictions, in common law countries, such as the United States, Canada, Australia, New Zealand, the UK or here in Ireland, it is prohibited for anyone other than a fully licensed lawyer to prepare legal documents of any kind for another person or entity. This is in the province of lawyers alone.

'As these descriptions show, lawyers almost always have a significant role to play in formal dispute resolution, no matter in which country they practise, but the specific tasks assigned to them tend to vary quite a bit. For example, a task outside the courtroom that is typically performed by lawyers in one country may be performed by skilled lay people in another. So remember, there are different approaches to providing and protecting rights and freedoms: we can assess objectively what the strengths and weaknesses are of the various approaches.

'It might be worth mentioning that in the UK and here in Ireland we have what is described as a "split legal profession", meaning that we have two sorts of lawyers:

barristers and solicitors. People may go directly to the solicitor, who would have an office on the High Street, whereas barristers traditionally work close to the courts in the Law Library or private offices or "chambers". They are the ones who stand up and argue cases in court. But I have covered a lot of detail, so we might return to this later.

'I was going to tell you a true story about how, in a common law setting, rights that we now take for granted were established in the past by an ordinary citizen. That is what we call "precedent". Let me introduce you to one – Ms May Donoghue. She and her friend went to a café one afternoon, in Paisley in Scotland, in August of 1928. First, let us imagine how they would have been dressed, so we can visualise the scene where the friend of Ms Donoghue ordered a "pear and ice-cream float" and for Ms Donoghue she ordered an "ice-cream and ginger beer". Ms Donoghue had enjoyed some of the ice-cream and ginger beer and then her friend poured the remainder of the ginger beer, which had come in a dark coloured bottle, into the tumbler and, as she did, out came a dead snail.'

'Oh no!' came the loud, horrified response. 'That is disgusting – really, a dead snail in the bottle?'

'Yes, that's what I said: the remains of a snail, in a state of decomposition, dropped out of the bottle into the tumbler before her eyes. Poor Ms Donoghue; she felt sick and vomited and that evening was most unwell with gastroenteritis and had ferocious headaches for a very long time.

'She tried to pursue a claim through the courts, but was unsuccessful at trial initially, but she then went on to appeal the decision to the House of Lords in the United Kingdom and finally, several years later, her claim was successful. In a nutshell, and apologies that this is in quite legal language, the appeal "was allowed", as they say, on the basis that manufacturers owe the final consumer of their product a duty of care (at least in the instance where the goods cannot be inspected between manufacturing and consumption, and the bottle was dark brown glass). The court's decision also said that there need not be a contractual relationship in order for the final consumer to sue in negligence.

'There you are; new law was made! The case of *Donoghue v Stephenson* (who was the manufacturer of the ginger ale) is also known as the "Snail in the Bottle Case" and is a very significant case in modern law. The ruling in this case established what is called the civil law tort of negligence. A tort is a wrongful act that causes a claimant to suffer loss or harm, resulting in legal liability for the person who commits the act. This ruling therefore obliged businesses to observe a duty of care towards their customers. As I said, this case took place in Paisley in Scotland in 1928 and the case was not finally decided by the House of Lords until 1932, so Ms Donoghue had to persevere and wait some time for her rights to be upheld. Now, lawyers being what they are, it will come as no surprise that many subsequent lawyers and academic commentators took issue with the decision in this case, mainly because Lord Atkin, who was the Law Lord who delivered the judgement, based his view and his conclusion on what is now described as the "neighbour principle". He was of the belief that a person is not to injure his neighbour by acts of negligence, and that certainly covers a very large field of law. He said he doubted whether the whole law of tort could not be comprised in the golden maxim "to do unto your neighbour as you would that he should do unto you".

'That's interesting because we were talking about that in the context of reasonableness and what our expectations are of other people. I remember being told that Lord Atkin discussed the case over lunch with his family when he was hearing the case and was interested in seeing the responses of his children when he was telling them the details of the case.'

'Not a good story to hear over lunch!' said Aver.

'As a matter of fact, poor Ms Donoghue had a very sad life after this case. Her life really was a bit of a tragedy, but she stands as a heroine because she did take a brave step in pursuing a right which we now all enjoy.'

As they walked around the outer areas of the courts through the corridors, observing the people coming and going, it became clear that people were wearing very odd-looking clothes. Dark suits were worn by both the men and the women. Judges who walked through at times making their way to their own court, led by their tipstaff, who was there to make sure that people did not block the judge's route, wore black cloaks over formal suits.

It was important to discuss with Mumu the different dress codes and traditions which are all part of the "symbols of justice".

'Well, how can I summarise it for you? All I can say to you is that these traditions go back a very long time and now, with the passing of time, and a number of reviews and requests to change and modernise the appearance of the courts, there have been some changes. Both here in Ireland in the UK you will see some people wearing black gowns and, in some instances, wigs. That can all be a bit confusing during this time of change, because there was, for example, a law that came in some years ago in Ireland saying that it was not compulsory for barristers to wear wigs while appearing in court but, unfortunately, some of the court rules, where it referred to "having a right of audience in a Court" – that is the right of the barrister to appear and address the court, on the client's behalf, still said that the barrister had to be "attired properly", and although it was not obligatory to wear wigs, some barristers continued to wear them when they were addressing the court. Then in 2011, a centuries-old tradition officially came to an end, when the then Chief Justice (the most senior judge), Mrs Justice Susan Denham, and most of her senior colleagues sat in the Supreme Court without their wigs for the first time.

'That old fashioned style which had been in place since the seventeenth century came to an end as a result of a decision of the Superior Court's Rules Committee, which included representatives of the judiciary, lawyers and the Courts Service.

'It was estimated that the change would save the State €2,200 (the cost of the unique horsehair wigs made in London, for each new judge appointed to the bench). The change was "signed into law" by the serving minister for justice.

'The compulsory wearing of wigs by barristers had been ended by the former Chief Justice but the gowns remained. Many barristers also chose to continue wearing wigs. The required form of address to a judge was also changed from "My Lord" to "Judge".

'The horsehair wigs, which have been worn in British courts as a matter of rule, tradition and law since the time of the restoration of the monarchy in the seventeenth century, survived the transition from the time when Ireland was under British rule to Irish independence in 1921 and thus we continued to wear them.'

'Are they heavy?' asked Aver.

'They are most uncomfortable.'

'Judges do not wear wigs in the United States, Canada, Australia, India or New Zealand, except on ceremonial occasions in the case of New Zealand. We must ask Verity if they do so in France.

'An exemption to the rule requiring wigs to be worn has existed for family law cases for some time, to minimise the formality associated with such cases, as well as in the Children's Court, where even members of the Garda Síochána – the police force – who are attending in the Children's Court will cover up their uniform with a more casual jacket.'

'Is that because they do not want the children to feel afraid?' asked Lex.

'Yes, it is policy that the surroundings should not appear too intimidating.

'So the general uniform is that barristers must wear a black or dark suit in court, the men with a waistcoat and the women with black jacket and matching skirt or tailored trousers or black dress, and they wear a shirt with a winged collar or the women may wear a rolled collar that can be worn with the white bands, which are the bands that the clergy have worn for hundreds of years.'

'Why were people slow to press for change?' asked Nova.

'I know that it seems odd to you, and all I can say is that people who work in this area believed that it created a level of formality and seriousness that is appropriate, given the nature of the cases that are heard in which people's lives will change considerably even in the civil cases, not to mention the criminal cases. I think that all of that formality was seen as a degree of respect for the process where the system of justice was "on view" and some believed that having it appear "different" emphasised the seriousness of the processes and the fact that our judicial system had survived for so long. I also heard it argued once that it provided a degree of disguise and security, especially for the judges, who would have appreciated not being recognised in their private lives when they had been involved in cases that were in the news.

'Of course, the world of the law has many stories about its quirks and traditions. One story was that if a barrister came in to court and, say for example, wore brown shoes with a black suit or did not wear a waistcoat (if it was a man), then the judge would just look down and say, "I don't hear you, Mr So and so; I don't hear you." That would be a way of bringing the barrister's attention to the fact that he was inappropriately attired and therefore did not have "a right of audience" in the court.'

'Does that mean that the judge would not "hear" what he had to say until he went away and came back dressed properly with his black shoes?' asked Aver, putting on a pompous voice.

'Well, you might ask me how women fared in this odd world. It took a very long time for women to gain some kind of equality as lawyers and a chance of having an equal opportunity of making a success of that career. Perhaps it would be helpful if we looked at how things are currently in Ireland. Exactly one-third of the judges are now women. Yes; the number of female judges in Ireland recently hit a "record high", making up exactly one-third of the judiciary, and recently a report from the Council of Europe showed that the systems with the lowest percentage of women among professional judges were Azerbaijan (11%), Armenia (23%), Northern Ireland (23%), Scotland (23%), England and Wales (30%) and Ireland (33%). The Europe-wide average was 51%. Also, it is worth mentioning that the European Court of Human Rights (ECHR) in Strasbourg has a relatively good record on gender diversity compared with most international courts, because currently seventeen out of the forty-seven ECHR judges are women, accounting for 36%. Another piece of interesting information, in what is a "first" for any legal profession in the world, is that female Irish solicitors outnumber male solicitors practising in Ireland. Recently, it was reported that just over ninety years ago the first woman solicitors were admitted to the profession and, since then, the race to equality has been rapid. I should have explained earlier that in Ireland, and in the UK, we have what we call a "split legal profession". That is to say, we have barristers, who are generally speaking the people who appear in court and "plead" the case, and solicitors, who are the people who have public offices and to whom the general public can go directly with their legal matters which may not require a barrister, such as drafting a will or drawing up a contract for some business. The Bar, which is the collective name for barristers, is overseen by the Bar Council, who have the oversight of barristers and have a "code of conduct", and the Law Society is the professional body that oversees the solicitors.

'There are some very interesting pieces of history about the first women to be "called to the Bar", which is the phrase we use when we talk about becoming a barrister. One was Ms Avril Deverill, who came from Greystones in County Wicklow. She became a barrister in 1921. It turns out she had driven an ambulance in France during the First World War. In 1919, the law changed to allow women to become barristers so, by 1921, she and one other woman, called Frances or Fay Kyle, had been admitted to the King's Inns in Dublin, and made history by becoming the first women to be called to the Bar in "the United Kingdom" (of which Ireland was then legally a part).

'It gives you some idea of the huge progress that women have made in the area of law in this country if you consider that the first woman to become a senior counsel was in 1977 – Ms Justice Mella Carroll, who then became the first female judge of the High Court in 1980. It is interesting also to consider the pressure that women were under, no matter how successful they appeared to be on the surface, because Judge Carroll later admitted that it took her ten years sitting on the Bench as a High Court judge to rustle up the courage to say that she didn't want to be called "Your Lordship" – as that implied that she was a man. Expressions such as "if it pleases Your Lordship" or "if Your Lordship pleases" all implied that the person sitting on the Bench was a man and she asked that she be addressed as "Judge" or referred to as the court, in the third person: "if it pleases the court".

'If I also tell you that up to about a year ago we had, in this relatively small country, the first female Chief Justice of the Supreme Court, which is the highest judge in the land. The Attorney General was a woman. The Chief State Solicitor was a woman. We had the Director of Public Prosecutions, also a woman, and we had had by that time two female Presidents, Mary Robinson being the first, followed by Mary McAleese, both of whom had been barristers.

'So now, I suppose to people of your generation you are looking at me and wondering why on earth I am making so much of this subject. But if you consider the approach and the attitude to women from not so long ago you would not be surprised.

'In order to illustrate this I found this interesting little book entitled *Learning the Law,* which we were all given when we started studying law. It was written by a man called Glanville Williams, who was the Rouse Ball Professor of English Law in the University of Cambridge. The ninth edition of this book came out in 1973, which is not really that long ago, and Professor Williams decided to name one of his chapters "Women", which, by the way, he relegated to the back of the book, and there is one passage I can remember every word of because I was so shocked when I read it that I have never forgotten it. In it Williams proclaimed:

> *'Practice at the Bar is a demanding task for a man; it is even more difficult for a woman.*
>
> *'In building up her practice at the Bar, a woman has a double prejudice to conquer: the prejudice of a Solicitor, and the prejudice of the Solicitor's lay client. It is not easy for a young man to get up and face the Court; many women find it harder still. An advocate's task is essentially combative, whereas women are not generally prepared to give battle unless they are annoyed. A woman's voice, also, does not carry as well as a man's.*

'This might give you an idea of how women at the Bar were viewed in the early 1970s.'

'Goodness, there are some singers who might not agree with that,' said Nova.

'Exactly,' the others chimed in unison.

'So just in case anybody thinks that we are lingering too long on this subject, I think it is worth just summarising several things that women could not do in the 1970s, notwithstanding the fact that all those famous emperors in ancient times used the symbol of the statue of Lady Justice to convey the impression of the importance and solidity of their judicial systems! So here is the summary:

'Firstly, a woman could not keep her job in the public service or a bank when she got married. The so-called "marriage bar" in the public service was eventually removed in July 1973, after the report of the Commission on the Status of Women and the new Employment Equality Act, which prohibited discrimination on the grounds of gender or marital status, in almost all areas of employment, came into law.

'Second, a woman could not sit on a jury under the 1927 Juries Act. Members of juries had to be property owners and, in effect, male. How did that change? Two women – Marín de Burca and Mary Anderson – challenged the Act and won their case in the Supreme Court in 1976. The old Act was repealed and all citizens over eighteen who were on the electoral register became eligible for juries. One of the lawyers representing the plaintiffs in this case, de Burca and Anderson, was Mary Robinson, who was later to become the first female President of Ireland. She was accompanied in that case by a very famous constitutional and human rights lawyer called Donal Barrington.

'So on top of that, a woman was not allowed to drink a pint in a pub. Yes, you are not hearing things! In the 1970s some pubs refused to allow women to enter at all, some allowed women only if accompanied by a man, and very many refused to serve women pints of beer. Women who were accidentally served a pint were told to pour it into two half-pint glasses. How did that change? Women's groups staged protests in the early 1970s. In one instance, the journalist Nell McCafferty led a group of thirty women who ordered, and were served, thirty brandies. Then they ordered one pint of Guinness. When the pint was refused, they drank the brandies and refused to pay, as their order was not served.

'In 2002 the Equal Status Act banned gender discrimination in the provision of goods and services. It defined discrimination here as "less favourable treatment". Service can be refused only if there is a reasonable risk of disorderly or criminal conduct. Another thing that a woman could not do in the 1970s was to collect her Children's Allowance. The 1944 legislation that introduced the payment of Children's Allowances (now called Child Benefit) specified that it be paid to the father. The father could, if he chose, mandate his wife to collect the money, but she had no right to it. How did that change? Responding to the report of the Commission on the Status of Women, the 1974 Social Welfare Act entitled mothers to collect the Allowance. That Commission on the Status of Women, I might add, was chaired by Mella Carroll, to whom we referred earlier as being the first female High Court judge in Ireland. There is a whole list of other things, such as getting a barring order against a violent partner, but this changed when Women's Aid campaigned for changes in the law in the Family Law Act, 1976 – Ireland's first legislation on domestic violence. This enabled one spouse to seek a "barring order" against the other where the welfare or safety of a spouse or children was at risk. That meant that the person was ordered to keep away from the house. The orders were for three months and were poorly implemented. In 1981 protection orders were introduced and barring orders increased up to twelve months. Believe it or not, a woman could not live securely in her family home under Irish law in those days because a married woman had no right to a share in her family home, even if she was the breadwinner. Her husband could sell the home without her consent. How did that change? Under the Family Home Protection Act of 1976, neither spouse could sell the family home without the written consent of the other. I could go on, but I will just end this list with one further thing that a woman could not do – and that was get the same rate of pay for a job as a man. In 1970 almost all women were paid less than male colleagues doing the same job.

'In March 1970 the average hourly pay for women was five shillings, while that for men was over nine shillings. In areas covered by a statutory minimum wage, the female rate was two-thirds that of men. This was changed by legislation on equal pay which was introduced in 1974, and employment equality legislation followed in 1977, but it is worth mentioning that both of these came in as a result of European directives.'

Five

The courts experience – evidence – the museum in a historical barracks – the futility of war

When the group was leaving the courts and heading towards the car, they reflected on the vast number of things that they had seen – from the symbols of justice, the large imposing hallways, people in very dark clothing walking back and forth, people who could be identified as judges, people who were barristers and solicitors, people who were clients, and even prisoners being escorted in and out by police officers. Mumu recalled that on the way back from the airport in the car someone had asked about evidence, and that was a subject to which she had intended to return.

'We might just talk a little about evidence. The question of evidence is important in criminal cases, and science has progressed so rapidly that evidence can be gathered much more comprehensively now than in the past. We all think about the obvious ways of taking fingerprints from a car door handle or from the front door where somebody has been accused of burgling or stealing, but what about

DNA fingerprinting, also known as genetic fingerprinting, and "DNA typing" and "DNA profiling", which enable identification of individuals using samples of hair, blood or other biological samples, based on unique patterns called polymorphisms in their DNA?

'All of the evidence which is used in court, especially the evidence obtained by scientific methods such as ballistics, blood tests and DNA tests, carries considerable weight. We have talked about the role of the police in gathering that information, and the role of the detective branch of the police force in particular in following up the investigations of any crimes.'

And as the group drove away from the Four Courts in the centre of Dublin on the north quays, Mumu suggested to them that they might think about the sorts of information that they would like to put in their notebooks, and the questions that they would like to ask Verity arising from what they had seen and discussed that day. In addition to asking questions, of course, it was important for them to note what they had seen that they might read up about later.

As they drove back across the River Liffey, Mumu decided it would be good to have a little break from legal matters so they headed down to a nearby section of the National Museum of Ireland in Collins Barracks, where there were a number of exhibitions. As they travelled, the two girls recognised where they were going and became very excited, recalling many visits to that place and the different exhibitions they had seen, which they in turn described to Rex and Lex. Mumu then explained briefly a little of the background to the museum.

'Collins Barracks is a former military barracks, originally called simply "The Barracks" and later "The Royal Barracks". The name was changed to Collins Barracks when it was handed over to the Irish Free State in 1922, following Irish independence. Housing both British armed forces and Irish army garrisons through three centuries, the barracks were the oldest continuously occupied example in the world. The buildings are now the National Museum of Ireland – Decorative Arts and History.

'Oh so you recognise the location? Well done,' Mumu said. At that point one of the girls excitedly remembered going to see the exhibition of the famous Irish-born designer and architect, Eileen Gray.

'I am not surprised that you recall that exhibition because of the fascinating designs. Yes, she was a very interesting woman – a noted innovator of her time. She was born in 1878 and died in October 1976. She was Irish, but mainly French-based during her later life. She is described as an architect and a furniture designer and a pioneer of the Modern movement in architecture. There are some iconic examples of her architectural skills shown in the homes that she built in the South of France.

'Do you remember the day that we visited this museum during the commemorations of the First World War and saw part of the project that they had called *Living History*? Remember, we saw the actors dressed in the exact uniforms of soldiers who would have been in the trenches in the First World War?'

'Oh, yes,' said Aver, 'I remember that.'

'Well, I'm going to guess what aspects of their presentation and the information they gave us you remember first!'

'Oh, Mumu, how can you remember that or guess what I am going to say?'

'Do you want to have a go and say what you remember that stands out from that experience, or shall I tell you what my guess is?'

'Okay, can you please tell me what your guess is,' said Aver.

'My guess is that you will recall one of the "soldiers" telling us about the terrible conditions of the soldiers in the First World War, who were living for so long in the filthy dirty trenches which were infested with rats and, of course, with fleas; and he described how the only way to get rid of the fleas from the uniform was to run a match down the seam. Then he mimicked on the sleeve of his uniform how running the match down would get rid of the fleas – but there were also unfortunate consequences of that. Can you imagine what they were?'

Next minute Aver interrupted and said: 'I remember.'

'Oh, so do I,' said Nova. 'May I describe it?'

'Well, let us not argue about our memories and the accuracy of them, but let us give an opportunity to Lex and Rex, who were not there with us. What would you think might be the consequences of doing that?'

Then, in a confident tone, Rex said that he thought that after running the flame down the seam several times, the threads would wither and the seam would come apart. Both of the girls were very impressed, although they did not let Rex see just how impressed they were. Aver added that she had thought many times since that day about how awful it would have been for those soldiers, whom she remembered were all so very young, trying to survive in those trenches – infested with rats and fleas, unable to wash or change their clothes for so long, not knowing when they would hear an explosion that could bring their lives to an end. Mumu could see that they were all getting a bit upset, so she began speaking.

'Yes, I think that a living history project is a very good idea because it helps us to imagine how things were for people in times past. Do you remember the day we went along and they had items of children's clothing from different generations far back in time, and the details that we were able to observe by handling a shoe that would have been made, maybe, in the eighteenth century?'

'Yes; it was very interesting, Mumu, and we were so glad you brought us there,' said Nova. 'I also remember the day that we went to the exhibition that showed us all of the items of war. What was that called? Oh, yes, that was called *Soldiers and Chiefs – the Irish at War at Home and Abroad from 1550 up to the present day.*'

Mumu then recalled it in more detail, saying that there were three sections. One was called *Soldiering at Home,* which showed us how Irishmen fought during the 1798 Rebellion, the Easter Rising of 1916, the War of Independence and the ensuing Civil War. Then there was *Soldiering Abroad,* which showed us how Irishmen and women fought for foreign armies in distant lands over the past five hundred years, and then there was the more up-to-date *Soldiering in the Twentieth and Twenty-first Centuries* – from the World Wars to the Irish Defence Forces' peace-keeping missions and role with the United Nations.

'Are there any women in the army in this country?' asked Rex.

'Yes, women were admitted as full members of the defence forces in 1992. At the moment, women account for about 6.5% of all of the personnel working in the army, naval service and air corps. That compares to the United States where the figures show that 16% of enlisted personnel are women, which is a rise from about 11% in 1990. Then in the UK, our nearest neighbour, some 9% of the armed forces are women.'

Now that Mumu was on that subject, she continued by saying that we should bear in mind that women do seem to have a comparatively good representation in this country and keep in line with trends internationally. She recalled the discussion about the number of women in the police force and the survey undertaken recently by the Council of Europe that showed that Sweden had the highest number, at 29.29%, and the UK had 27% of women in the police force and Ireland was not too far behind at 25%.

'Remember that we also discussed the very high representation of women in the legal profession, which is the core of our project.'

'Yes,' they all said.

'But all these other things about the law and the way that the law works are very interesting to us because they help us to understand how society was changing over the years and how the rules have to come in line with the needs of a new society,' said Nova, in a most enthusiastic tone.

As they drove up the long approach to the National Museum of Ireland, Mumu added a little bit more background information by saying, 'Ireland is often discussed regarding its struggle for freedom from the control of the British, which, as we know, was commemorated in 2016 – being the hundredth anniversary of what we call the Easter Rising, leading to the independence of this state, which a few years later led to further bitter fighting and bloodshed in the Civil War that followed.

'But it is often forgotten that Irish soldiers played a part in the First World War and Second World War. People do not agree totally on the numbers, but at least 49,000 Irish soldiers died in the First World War, as recorded by the National War Memorial, and it is said that between 140,000 and 210,000 Irish soldiers volunteered to serve in the British army between 1929 and 1945, in spite of the fact that during that time Ireland had gained its independence from the United Kingdom. It is said that as many as 10,000 lost their lives in the Second World War.

'As regards female participation, it is recorded that 16% of all British military nurses who were killed were Irish. There are, of course, differing views of history, but not so long ago a Trinity College historian called Dr Stephen O'Connor published a book on Irish officers in the British forces between 1922 and 1945, and he estimated that 77,000 Irishmen served in British uniform during the Second World War. Of course, it is important to bear in mind that these soldiers would have volunteered, not been called up by conscription, which is the process requiring young men of at least eighteen years of age to serve in the defence of a country in time of war. (Conscription was never extended to Ireland by the British authorities in relation to the First World War.)

'I read another account recently that said that 4,468 soldiers from Southern Ireland (which is what they called this country), who were killed in the Second World War, were joined by some 4,000 soldiers from Northern Ireland who were killed in action. It is difficult when we are discussing this subject because we have to bear in mind that Ireland was a neutral country and was not a colonial power. It never invaded any other territory so, in that context, the fact that so many people decided to volunteer and serve alongside their neighbours in the British army is a very significant factor in our history, which I think we should always acknowledge.'

Somehow, the conversation having drifted back to war again, it was time to take a break. In the quadrangle, which would have been the barracks parade ground, there is a café, so Mumu decided that some cool drinks were in order.

Everybody selected their drinks and Lex ran outside to find a free table. They all sat outside for a while and then Nova suggested that they line up in the centre of the main barracks square. She directed them to space out evenly and then she started to shout out orders, telling them to take giant steps forward as she tried to get them to move in unison. When they reached the wall Nova shouted, 'About turn!' She varied the pace and the instructions on the return march, her small voice echoing through the cloisters.

Mumu was lost in thought, triggered by the group emulating military formations – images which they would probably have seen in films. She pondered on the responsibilities of handing on a perception of military history that could carry with it a presumption of inevitable repetition. Her thoughts were heavy as she recalled the coverage of the recent centenary commemorations of the Battle of Passchendaele, also known as the Third Battle of Ypres, fought during the First World War.

The group ran back to finish their drinks.

'I have just been thinking here about a famous and unique man for several reasons, but mainly because we have been talking about armies and we are here in what was once a military barracks,' said Mumu.

'Last year was the centenary commemoration of one of the worst battles of the First World War – the Battle of Passchendaele, fought in Belgium. It went on for ninety days and some 3,000 soldiers in the British army were lost every day.

'I know something about it because I have seen documentaries about a man who recalled and described vividly being in those trenches in the mounds of mud. His name was Harry Patch, and he was the last surviving British soldier of the First World War. He died on Saturday 25 July 2009, in a care home in Somerset, at the age of 111. He was known as "The Last Tommy". A Tommy was the nickname for the lowest rank of ordinary soldier. Harry Patch was nineteen years old when he was in that trench defending the Western Front from attack by the advancing German army.

'I saw one documentary about a time when he had travelled back to France in 2005, when he was aged 107. He said in that film that war was a calculated act to condone the slaughter of human beings and he said that war was a "licence to murder". The story is that he did not talk about his First World War experiences until he turned 100 years old. Then he devoted his time to spreading the message about the evil and futility of war and became an anti-war hero. He said that he had tried for eighty years to forget the horror but that he could not do so. He arranged to meet the last surviving German soldier and he paid a visit to the cemetery where the fallen German soldiers had been buried. Four million soldiers had fought on that Western Front.

'He expressed his views so simply from his own personal experience. A shell had exploded when he and his close friends were returning from the front line and three had perished. He was injured but somehow survived. In one scene he is sitting in his wheelchair in a section of the cemetery, where 8,000 unidentified soldiers are buried – hoping that perhaps his three friends might be among these graves – and he reflects on their loss.'

At this point Mumu called up the film clip on her phone and they watched the part where Harry Patch is looking at the memorial inscribed with all the names. The film shows him then visiting the German cemetery, where 40,000 German soldiers are buried. He asks to take two acorns from the earth, which he plans to plant when he returns home, and the film shows his doing this with the words, 'They will grow.'

Mumu became moved at this memory. Nova and Aver noticed and Nova put her arms out to console her, but could not hide the tears that were dropping down her own cheeks.

'Oh, Mumu, why can't we all share this world together

equally and make the most of it? There's only one world.'

By this time they were all getting upset and Mumu apologised. She told them that she now felt guilty because, of course, this was only one huge war and there are millions of people all over the world who have suffered, and are now suffering, from all the pain of wars, oppression, terrorism and injustice. She explained that she was moved by the simple words Harry Patch had used, and that she had often wondered how it had been for him to have witnessed the cycle of war repeating again during the Second World War (1939–1945). She wondered if he had ever spoken about that. She told the group that she was thinking about the repetition of wars when they were playing.

'Do you think that people listen to anti-war heroes like Harry Patch?' asked Rex.

'Well, that is what I mean, Rex. Sometimes it seems that people close their minds to words of experience and wisdom.'

'Yes, but people know that what that man was saying makes sense, so why would they allow all those things to happen again? It just does not make sense,' Nova added in an exasperated voice.

'But we are to grow too, like those acorns Harry Patch planted,' said Aver, bringing a tone of optimism to the discussion.

Six

The Great Irish Famine – the Corn Laws – famine ships – the poetry of Yeats – planning the penfriend project

'Sometimes it is very important to look at law through a wider lens, both in the present day and significantly in the past, and see when there were times when laws acted against the interests of the general public and brought great hardship and misery to many people. In many respects, the application of good laws is about providing and protecting the human rights of the people who live in the country of those laws, or in other countries or territories where those laws were extended in times of colonial power, when nations such as Great Britain, and others, colonised other territories and imposed their laws on the local people.'

Mumu was driving along the north side of the River Liffey, passing what is now called the *Famine Memorial,* a set of sculptures commissioned by Norma Smurfit in 1997 and presented to the City of Dublin in that year. These sculptures are a commemorative work dedicated to those Irish people forced to emigrate during the 1840s

Irish Famine. The sculptures were designed and crafted in bronze by Dublin sculptor Rowan Gillespie and are located on Custom House Quay, in the heart of Dublin docklands. Mumu was unable to pull in, but she drove as slowly as she safely could as the group peered out the window, looking back as they drove past at the statues that depicted the desperation of famine.

'The location is a particularly appropriate and historic one because one of the very first voyages of the famine period was on a ship called the Perseverance, which sailed from the Custom House Quay on St Patrick's Day in 1846. The captain of the ship was called William Scott, a native of the Shetland Islands. He had given up his office job in New Brunswick to take the Perseverance out of Dublin at a time when he was 74 years old.

'The "steerage" or passenger fare was £3, which at that time was a lot of money. It is said that 210 passengers made that historic journey, landing in New York on 18 May 1846. Just think of that time – from St Patrick's Day, 17 March, to 18 May – two months on that ship and, miraculously, all passengers and crew survived the journey. That was not always the case. Indeed, many of those poor emigrants died en route because when they started the journey they were in such bad physical shape that there was very little strength to sustain all the challenges of such a long journey.

'If you ever get the chance to see inside one of those ships you will get an idea of the conditions in which they lived and the way they slept "head to toe", cramped in down below board, with very little fresh air and, in some instances, no fresh air, because the captain would not let them up to the top deck.

'When I had a tour of the one of the famine ships called the Jeanie Johnston, the guide who was giving us the history of that ship (a replica of one built in Canada in

1847) recalled a particular captain who did allow some of the people to go up in small groups to get some fresh air. Can you suggest why fresh air would be so important?'

'Oh yes,' was the overall answer from the group.

'Well, you all seem to have many suggestions; let's hear them,' Mumu replied.

'Well, they would need to have oxygen in their lungs, otherwise they would be stifled if they were stuck down below,' said Rex.

'And they would need some sunlight on their skin for their bones,' said Aver.

'Yes, that's very good,' said Mumu, 'you've covered most of the reasons. And, of course, one of the great problems on those journeys was that the passengers did not have very much to eat so they would have been craving vitamin C, which they could get from oranges, and they needed some calcium from milk but, of course, their diet was really bad.'

'How many people died at that time, Mumu?' asked Lex.

'Well, it is estimated that at least one million people died from starvation and all the diseases that followed from the famine, and a further one million people emigrated. They took their chances on those ships. So, overall, it was a devastating time for Ireland because the population of the island dropped from over eight million in 1845 to about six million in 1850. You can just imagine the significance of that for a small country.

'The catastrophic famine of the 1840s devastated Ireland, an event, in the words of Mary Robinson (the first woman President of Ireland), "which more than any other shaped us as a people. It defined our will to survive. It defined our sense of human vulnerability."'

'Oh no,' chimed all of the group, 'how could something so terrible happen?'

'It discloses a very complex and controversial time in history; what happened, in a nutshell, was that the potato crop, on which a very large number of the population depended, failed because it was hit by a blight – a type of disease. There just was no other food here – for many historical and local reasons – and particularly because of laws at that time, known as the Corn Laws.'

'What were they?' asked Lex.

'They were tariffs, charges, and other trade restrictions on imported food and grain such as corn, which were enforced by Great Britain between 1815 and 1846. They were designed to keep grain prices high in order to favour their own local domestic producers – which, at that time, was said to represent British "mercantilism". Maybe at another time we can look that up and find out what that means in terms of economics and the running of a country. But those Corn Laws imposed heavy import duties, making it very expensive to import grain from abroad even when food supplies were running out.

'Without getting into too much detail – because this is turning into a bit of a history lesson more than a review of legal processes – the Corn Laws really increased the profits and power associated with land ownership – and, of course, remember that at that time Ireland was under British rule and large parts of Ireland were owned by English landlords who had been sent over and given land in Ireland. As a result of the Corn Laws, food prices were high and the consequences, as I have described, were catastrophic in Ireland. We must also bear in mind that poor people in Britain had been adversely affected by the resulting high cost of food, so there had been a lot of social unrest and rioting around the country and protests at the Parliament over there. There is a poem called "Quarantine" by Irish poet Eavan Boland which expresses many things in a short space with urgent words that basically remind us all that we should never forget the levels of strength and survival and near-to-the-edge dispossession that we once had as a people. It is a very dark and sad poem that I would recommend you wait until you are a little older to read. I believe that the only good that can come out of recalling cruel times in history is to honour the innocent and unidentified victims and heroes who stood up to protect the vulnerable, but also to build our resolve to work, even in the smallest ways in our everyday lives, to prevent such events being repeated.'

Mumu looked through the rear-view mirror and saw that her students were becoming quite tired, so she decided to take the car in another direction. They crossed over to the south side of the city, and drove up towards the street where the Irish Parliament is located, which has, on one side of it, part of the National History Museum and, on the other side, the National Library. They drove into a nearby car park and the passengers recognised where they were going, so Mumu announced, with some enthusiasm:

'I think we've had a lot of hard work today so I am sure people are feeling a little bit like a rest now and possibly something to eat.'

'Oh yes, please, yummmmmm,' was the response, followed by, 'Thank you very much, Mumu, that would be really great.'

Mumu was smiling, but she also had another plan in mind. As they came to the traffic lights, she suggested that just before they go in and have that well-deserved snack, they might do something to relax everybody, so that they could enjoy their food all the more after all the discussions of loss and conflict. She saw the traffic lights turn green. Everyone was looking right and left and proceeded across the road to what was the National Library of Ireland.

The girls were not apprehensive because they knew already what they were heading towards, and that was a wonderful exhibition of the writings of the poet William Butler Yeats. Mumu explained that William Butler Yeats, who was widely considered one of the greatest poets of the English language, had received the 1923 Nobel Prize for Literature, and that his work was greatly influenced by the heritage and politics of Ireland.

Rex was looking a little bit hesitant, but Nova and Aver told him about the exhibition; they had seen it before, so they knew all about it.

Mumu had decided that they were certainly not going to try to take in the whole of this exhibition, which is well worth doing, but she took them to a central area cordoned off in a circular shape with a circular bench permanently in place upon which visitors could sit, surrounded by images of some of the most famous poems of Yeats. In front was a screen on which these images were reflected, with the titles and words of some of those poems which were being read, in sequence, by some famous recorded voices.

So Mumu sat down with her tired band of learners and soon all were relaxed and melted in to the beautiful bewitching sounds of some of the most famous Yeats poems. When the cycle of readings was finished, she signalled to go and they headed quietly out the door. Everyone was now smiling and looking happy. They crossed the road, and headed to the side entrance of this place that Aver had said was her most favourite place in the whole world when she was smaller. Very soon everybody had looked at the menu and made their choice of favourite sandwich and either apple juice or a glass of milk. As they were making their choices, Mumu had said, 'If anyone is interested, my favourite Yeats poem is "He wishes for the cloths of heaven".'

'I remember that, Mumu!' said Nova.

'I am so glad you remember that because I gave it to you to read when you were very small, and you read it in such a sensitive tone although you were only five, I was astonished!'

Mumu realised that the enthusiasm of the group for this project was quite astonishing in itself and she did not want to put too much pressure on their young minds, so she said: 'Look, we can just sit here munching away at our delicious food or you can ask questions or I can ask you questions about what you made of our experiences so far today. But because it has really been an action-packed day, we could just sit here and talk about nothing in particular or not talk at all!'

'Oh that is a good idea!' they said as they looked over their sandwiches and laughed heartily.

'Well,' added Aver through the laughter, 'we have done a lot of thinking and a lot of listening and you have been doing a lot of talking and explaining, Mumu, so maybe it is a time for a rest!'

'Okay, I agree,' said Mumu, 'but what I do ask is that you will all agree that this evening when you get home you will write down some of the thoughts or questions that you have had so far.'

'Oh, I have questions written already,' said Aver.

'Yes, I have as well,' said Rex,

'Oh, Lex, do you have any questions written down?'

'No,' he said, rather hesitantly, 'but I do have them all in my head.'

'That's fine. Tonight can you put those down in your notebook? Then the next thing is for all of you to vote who will be in charge of gathering together all the topics and questions for this project.'

'Oh, Mumu, we've already taken that vote,' was the united answer.

'We have decided that Nova will be the person for that job; she will come back to us and ask us what questions we would like to put to Verity in the first of the penfriend project letters.'

'I think we need to put a bit of a time limit and shape on this; do you agree?' asked Mumu.

'Yes we do,' was the response

'Could we plan it that there might be one letter every four weeks? Would that be manageable?'

'Yes,' was the answer from everyone.

So it was agreed that one letter would go to Verity every four weeks and, during times of school tests, or any other heightened activity, that might have to stretch to six weeks, but they would aim to have one communication every month going over to France and hopefully then receive a reply from Verity in response.

Seven

Young people and the law – diversionary programmes – rehabilitation and restorative justice – keeping people out of the courts and out of prison

It was over a week before Mumu met her group again. In many ways it had been quite difficult for some of the younger ones to fully understand the concepts that were being discussed, but Nova and Aver were still very keen to keep the project going and they had not run out of questions to ask or ideas for the penfriend project.

This time the meeting took place down by the sea quite close to where Mumu lived. There is a lovely walkway there along the front, like a promenade from the olden days, which makes its way around to a tiny beach on a corner and then up a slight hill towards the Forty Foot – an interesting bathing place where people can go down on the rocks to swim in the sea. A short distance further on, there is a beautiful panoramic view across Dublin Bay to Howth, which is directly across the bay from where they were in Sandycove, near Dalkey – a small fishing village on the southern outskirts of Dublin.

As they walked around the corner they passed by the Joyce Tower – an old Martello Tower now used as a commemorative centre for the famous Irish writer, James Joyce. Admission is free and memorabilia can be viewed and information obtained about the life of James Joyce.

At various times of the year famous actors come and read pieces from his novels for the enjoyment of the general public. As the group walked along, the tide was out a little so they could see the rocks, and they discussed lots of things, like the formation of the rocks, and everybody agreed that when the tide was in you had no idea about the sharp rocks that lay just beneath the surface. This unseen danger presented a real hazard for people swimming there or indeed in any part of the world where rocks lay near the shore.

As they passed along they came upon a number of lifebuoys in little wooden frames that could be used to throw out to somebody who was in distress. Underneath these was a sign reading: 'If you steal or damage this you could be taking a life', so this led to a discussion which was opened by Nova about crime and punishment and the cycle of crime.

'What do you do with young people?' she asked. 'Should young people who steal things be sent to prison? Are there special prisons for young people? What else could you do with people who do bad things?'

'Well, as you know, the age of seven is considered by some people as the "age of the use of reason"; so a child of seven is expected to know the difference between right and wrong and between good and bad.'

'Yes, Mumu, but that is not always the case, and it depends on the child!'

'Yes, I understand; you are so right. The facts are that children are among the most vulnerable members of society. The law of a country usually protects children until they are considered able to interact in society as adults. For this reason, children are treated differently from adults by the criminal justice system. The word "child" itself is now generally accepted to mean a person under the age of eighteen years in many countries. Speaking from memory, the age of criminal responsibility in our country was recently raised by a new law from seven years of age to twelve years of age. This means that children who have not reached the age of twelve years cannot be charged with an offence. However, there is an exception for children aged ten to eleven, who can be charged with murder, manslaughter, rape, or aggravated sexual assault. In addition, where a child under fourteen years of age is charged with an offence, no further proceedings can be taken without the consent of the Director of Public Prosecutions. You will recall that I mentioned that that office is currently occupied by a female, when we were talking about the number of women holding high office in the area of the law.

'That office is in charge of deciding on the prosecution of offences. So in the case of a charge against a child, the Director of Public Prosecutions will take special interest in making sure that the child is properly treated and legally represented.

'Although the law in general prohibits children under twelve years of age from being charged and convicted of a criminal offence, they do not have total immunity from action being taken against them. Under the law, there is a responsibility on the Gardaí (the police) to take a child under twelve years of age to his or her parents or guardian where they have reasonable grounds for believing that the child has committed an offence with which the child cannot be charged, due to the child's age. Where this is not possible, the Gardaí will arrange for the child to be taken into the custody of what is known as the Child and Family Agency (there are equivalents in our neighbouring countries) for the area in which the child normally resides. It is possible that children under twelve years of age who commit criminal offences would be dealt with by such an agency and not by the criminal justice system.

'Just to explain what I mean by that, there are lots of programmes and pilot schemes which have been invented to try and find ways of keeping children and young offenders out of the criminal justice system. They do this very well in Scotland, where they are known to have taken a lead in the area of education and youth affairs. So there are programmes which involve specially trained Gardaí in this country who are called juvenile liaison officers (JLOs), who have special arrangements for cautioning children in front of their parents during specially convened meetings. These meetings put the child at the centre of a discussion, with the parents present, and the realities of their bad behaviour are put to them with a very clear description of what the consequences will be if they do not stop behaving badly. This is an attempt to try and provide young children – who might be hanging out with the wrong kinds of people and turning towards a life of bad behaviour, or public order misbehaviour – with a chance to avoid being put through the courts system.

'They call them diversionary programmes in Scotland, where they have local schemes dealing with petty crime in communities where specially trained people bring the parties together. For example, if children have been vandalising somebody's garden or causing some sort of damage, these people try to intervene and bring about a situation where everybody finds a way of encouraging, persuading and guiding the young people away from the kind of behaviour which, if unchecked, could later turn into serious public order offences. So, with young people especially, the idea is to try to keep them out of the criminal justice system because of what they call the "revolving door" pattern that I told you about before.

'Under special laws dealing with children, a court may impose a period of detention on a child, but where that child is under sixteen years of age, the child is placed in a special detention centre or school. Generally speaking, the laws about children and crime are based on the philosophy that children in conflict with the law should only be detained – kept in custody – by the State as a very last resort. So there are many community-based measures which must be explored and tried before detention can be considered.

'This brings us to a much wider and very serious subject about the concept of crime and punishment, and the question which is never fully answered is: "What are the main objectives and benefits of keeping people in prison?" Some people would argue that it is a waste of public resources, except in cases where the person in question is a threat to society, and that it is only when a person actually poses such a threat that they should be kept in a prison. It is quite a controversial subject, but most people believe that, for both young and older people, rehabilitation is important. That means providing prisoners with opportunities they need – helping people who have not had sufficient education or training to pursue their education or learn new skills, or providing access to drug treatment programmes for people who have been on drugs. The challenge is to engage these people sufficiently so that they can, in turn, engage with society and get a job whenever their sentence is up. Getting a job after a person has been in prison is not an easy thing to do and that is really a chapter in itself because people are very unlikely to give a job to somebody who has "served time", as it is called.'

'Why is that, Mumu?' asked Lex.

'Can you think why that might be the case, Lex?'

'Because they think that they might do bad things while they are working for them?'

'Yes, exactly.'

'What about people turning over to being good when they are in prison; is that possible? What do you think about that, Mumu?' asked Aver.

'There is a lot to say about that subject, Aver, because there are so many famous cases of people doing just that: getting an education, studying for particular qualifications, learning a craft or learning a skill while they have been in prison. It is important that countries provide sufficient resources to give people lots of those options while they are "serving time". And yes, there have been many cases of people who did very bad things and then wrote books describing their experiences, all in a way to try and get the message across, especially to younger people in the outside world, about the consequences of going "down the criminal road" and advising people of the losses and suffering it brings on whole families. These people try to show, through their time of imprisonment, the truth about a life of crime, and they share that with other people who might have thought that it is "cool" or "macho" to be seen in that kind of role.'

'What does macho mean, Mumu?' asked Aver.

'It's a word which is short for *machismo,* which could be described as "the brandishing of male aggressive features" that some boys put on to act tough. Some think that being a "tough guy" is attractive; but others are intimidated by that. Some males think that if they do not behave in that way they might be vulnerable, so in order to keep in with the gang, they behave in a macho way out of intimidation and fear.'

Mumu walked on around the corner from the Forty Foot swimming area and everybody was quiet for a minute. The group were thinking about what they had been discussing.

All of a sudden Nova said, 'What about people with no chance in life, Mumu? Do you think crime is linked to the level of resources and support that people have?'

'Well, Nova, I can understand why people might jump to that conclusion, and many believe that there is research there to show that is the case. Over time, some research suggests that people from disadvantaged areas, as we sometimes call them – which can be demeaning for many people who live there – or people who have had a deprived life, or a life of suffering, or a life of ill-treatment, tend to end up with limited opportunities themselves. But we must be careful not to categorise people or to make assumptions. Many people overcome the challenges of their circumstances and many who have had many advantages in life waste their opportunities and end up doing bad things, so we must be ever cautious about labelling people as if they are somehow to blame for their lives. We have to look at the structures of our society in general to study the causes of anti-social behaviours.

'Without getting too political or going into it in too much detail, if we look critically at our housing policies, our town planners and the way large housing developments were built, even at a time when there was plenty of money in the public purse, we will find that they were usually built far away from public transport, without locally accessible amenities. There were no nurseries or crèches, no sports grounds, no playgrounds and no youth clubs providing activities for teenagers and young adults. All these amenities are so important and there are many people – some volunteers – who have devoted their time to setting up community sports clubs because they believe so strongly in the need for sports for young people. Most people will agree that the greatest dangers for young people are when they are just "hanging around", because they are vulnerable to approaches from people involved in selling drugs who would have devious ways of getting them involved in their activities and "grooming" them, as it is called.'

'We had talks in school about drugs and the way young people get drawn in to being involved,' said Nova.

'So did we,' echoed the others.

'Well, then you know something about the threats. It is important not to think of those threats as being only for people in certain sections of society because, as we mentioned already, even some people who are privileged to be in colleges and universities get involved with drugs, and recent reports about campus life paint a very worrying picture. Oh dear, we are discussing some of the serious sides of life for young people – but the whole subject of short-sighted planning for society's welfare and environmental requirements needs to recognised.

'Even before the recession of about ten years ago, which was linked to the unrealistic rise in property prices, when there was a lot of spending, developers were putting up very poor-quality housing and apartment blocks with poor quality materials, no thought to energy-saving heating schemes or domestic storage for growing families, just putting them up as cheaply as possible without ensuring their durability, environmental safety or other standards.

'So, we need to ask what was in the minds of the governments, local councils, architects, town planners, environmental inspectors, and the people who created those buildings. Did they ever consider how people were going to come and go? How far would they have to travel to go to a shop? What would they do with small children and teenagers and young adults? What after-school facilities were available? Indeed, how could they get to and from school?

'Then, during the recession years, they all forgot to think about the population that was growing in the meantime. The developers stopped building and our governments did not maintain any kind of adequate housing programmes, the result of which is that we have suddenly "woken up" to the fact that we are in the midst of a serious social problem with no accommodation for thousands of families. It was as if they thought that everyone would emigrate in the time of the recession and there would be no growth in our population.'

'Surely, they could count the people,' said Nova.

'So, there will be lots of people asking about that when candidates are looking for votes in the next election,' Aver said in a heavy sarcastic voice.

'And, as you can imagine, when the problem is at such a serious level, it is difficult to find sustainable solutions without making more "quick-fix" mistakes,' said Mumu.

'We are wandering off our subject a bit but you are right to make all those social connections and ask those questions. One matter that is universally accepted is the basic need for literacy, because that is the essential tool that children need early in life – the ability to read and write; so we must always support programmes that aim to give basic education to children all over the world.'

'I saw a report on the news about that, Mumu,' said Nova. 'It was about the growing number of refugee camps, with all the migration, and they were discussing the fact that children in the camps were without any schooling.'

'Oh, Mumu, some problems just seem too big to fix,' said Lex.

'It seems like that at times, but we just need to come up with creative solutions to smaller local matters and hope that we can apply those on a wider scale.'

'Yes, I suppose, it is all about sharing knowledge, isn't it? And we must keep trying,' said Lex.

'But why do those in charge of us keep making the same mistakes?' said Rex. 'They do not seem to learn from past mistakes. Remember when we were talking about anti-war heroes and how another world war happened after the first one.'

'I wish I could answer that, but I cannot do so and I am not going to throw out platitudes or meaningless suggestions. You are all looking at me now for using another new word (platitudes) and I think you should all look it up later. It is hard to have discussions like this with young people because sometimes there is a temptation to say that we are all relying on you – the new generation – to come up with new ways and solutions. And, of course, that is hardly fair because you can look at us and say that we did not make a very good job of coming up with solutions to social and universal problems. But I hope, from our discussions about the principles of justice, you can see how many have contributed to creating protections for peoples' rights. Just think of Ms Donoghue, all dressed up in her Sunday best, and how her encounter with the snail in her Sunday treat led to a change in the law protecting consumers' rights all those years ago.'

At that the group began to laugh.

'Shall we return to our main topic? There are lots of different ways of looking at the problem of young offenders and how to handle the problem; it is a complicated area. For example, there is a process described as 'restorative justice', which basically means that you bring the victim and the person who has done the bad thing together, to see whether the person who has done the bad deed can understand the suffering and the fear and the loss suffered by the person against whom they committed their crime. And then you wonder, Can they really feel sorrow and regret and can they make a full apology? Will that make any difference to the person who was the victim? Will it in any way undo the harm? Will it help them to get over the fear and the hurt and the loss that they have sustained? I know a little bit about this subject because I have heard experts in the area give lectures on it.

'A very well-known person from Dublin, who had worked for many years in Scotland on such programmes, used to give a guest lecture to the postgraduate course, *Conflict and Dispute Resolution Studies* in Trinity College Dublin, that I established some years ago. I always listened with great interest to the progress of ideas about restorative justice programmes. But the reality is that sometimes it works and sometimes it fails. It is a very cost-intensive area because it requires very highly skilled people to bring the victim of a crime together with the perpetrator and to handle that, because there is a great risk of it going wrong and of the person who was the victim perhaps being "victimised" all over again by coming face to face with the realities of what had been done to them and further hurt by that experience.'

'What about young people who steal cars and then crash them and then set them on fire?' said Lex. 'This is so destructive because then there is nothing left, only a burning wreck of a car. I saw that on television once.'

'Yes, that is called joy-riding. I always thought that was an interesting use of words. I used to ask myself the question, "Where is the joy?" But then that is me asking the question from my perspective, Lex. We have to see things from the mind of the people who are doing them in the context of their lives. So for those young boys, and they are usually males, who do it, it seems to give them some sort of a thrill. It seems to excite them and make them feel powerful in some way that they can take something that belongs to somebody else, drive it at great speed, and then take pleasure in destroying it and seeing it burn – although we might find it hard to see what excitement they would get from seeing something being destroyed.

'This conversation is reminding me of something that I experienced some years ago when I was a member of a charity called the Irish Youth Foundation. It used to raise money and then provide grants to groups of teachers or local community leaders – a variety of people – who had interesting ideas to help young offenders who were finding it very hard to get out of the cycle of unemployment. Every year there used to be an exhibition of all of the groups who had received grants so we could go to see for ourselves what they had come up with.

'For example, I remember one teacher in a city in Ireland who had created a small chocolate-making factory where young girls who had got into trouble with petty crimes like shoplifting were able to put their energy into making specialist chocolates and see them being valued.

'One man, whose stand really impressed me, was a car enthusiast, and like you, Lex, he could not understand why young men, who usually like cars and are fascinated by the design of sports and other kinds of cars, would think it fun to steal cars, smash them and then set them on fire. He was a mechanic and he used to restore cars. He was also a collector of cars, in a small way. He was not a wealthy man but he wanted to try and contribute to stopping this "cycle of crime", so he had an idea to set up a workshop beside his garage where he took apart old sports cars and then he invited boys who had come out of young offenders' detention centres to rebuild the cars, with small groups of them working together in teams.

'It was a very detailed and drawn-out process but his hope was that the boys would become so intrigued by and interested in the structure of the cars that they would learn to value them while they learned new skills and saw the time, care, and patience that was needed in actually constructing those vehicles.'

'I wonder how many of those boys did change their ways after that experience,' said Rex.

Mumu did not have an exact answer other than to recall that the project had been referred to as a success, but Nova suggested that if even one boy was inspired to change his ways by the project then it would have been worthwhile.

summons, they are all called "written pleadings". So, in other words, pleading is the interaction – the submissions and responses to the accusations or to the claims, that are part of the formal dialogue of the court process. Do you remember we were discussing the difference in the French court system, where the judge was more of an investigator or an inquisitor, looking into things and extracting information and evidence, whereas in Ireland and in the UK and other common law jurisdictions such as the United States, Canada, Australia and New Zealand, the lawyers stand in front of the court, and face the judge and submit the points and arguments on behalf of their clients? All those arguments are "the pleadings".

'This is how the word is used in court, and in a criminal case where somebody is going to be sentenced or where they have been accused of some crime, even a petty crime, there is an opportunity to put a "plea" to the court – for the lawyer representing the person to say why the judge should be lenient and not give them a harsh sentence or the sort of sentence that they normally would. So when they put a plea they are actually asking the court to consider special exemptions or special conditions for their client because of their personal circumstances.

'So if a boy stole seven apples from the orchard of a very wealthy man and he was caught doing so by a neighbour and brought to the police and, ultimately, to the Children's Court, and the judge asked him why he had done this and what defence he had, if any, and if that boy said back to the judge, on his own behalf, or through his lawyer, that he had four siblings at home and there was very little money at the moment because only one of the parents had a job, and that sometimes they were hungry in the evenings, making an apple very welcome, so that boy had stolen the apples to bring them back to his family. What do you think the judge should do about this? That is a "plea of mitigation". Is it enough to encourage the judge to let the boy go and not give him any punishment?'

'Oh yes, Mumu,' said Nova enthusiastically.

'Well yes, that is a good response, Nova, but what about the person who owns the orchard?'

'Oh dear, that's a tough one, Mumu!'

'What about people who sell drugs to young people? What should happen to them? Is that any worse than being a burglar or a pickpocket?

'So, you will see there are crimes against property and against the person. If a burglar enters your house then they are damaging your property and they are stealing your property. A pickpocket takes money out of your purse, your wallet, or out of your pocket. But if a mugger hits you or attacks you to steal from you, that is physical assault, so that is a crime against the property *and* the person.

'What about people who set fire to a forest or break up the swings in a playground or, as we referred to just a few minutes ago, take a lifebuoy out of its bracket? Really, what I am trying to get you to think about at this stage is the element of premeditation.'

'Oh, Mumu, that's another big word.'

'Well, it is not really. "Pre" means something that went before and "meditation" is to think about something, so if you put them together you get the picture. In other words, somebody who plans to break into a house, somebody who looks at a buoy in its bracket and says, "I know that is there to save somebody's life if they are in difficulties at sea but I am going to take it out and I am going to hide it or break it' – that would be premeditated; they know what they are going to do. They might say, "I'm going to go up to that man because his wallet is sticking out of his back pocket and I am going to take that wallet, as I brush past him, and perhaps distract him to look to the left while I put my hand over to his right pocket."'

'That makes me remember *Oliver* the musical that we went to see once in the National Concert Hall, so we know what a pickpocket is. We know how they operate,' said Aver.

'If you steal a car or a bicycle or a mobile phone or somebody's wallet, it is taking something that does not belong to you, and when you are doing it you know that you are doing it, and you have started to do it with the intention of taking something away; that's really the definition of stealing – or larceny, as it used to be called. It is the unlawful taking of the personal property of another person or a business. It was an offence under the common law and became an offence in jurisdictions which incorporated the common law, as we discussed before.

'The actual term "larceny" has been abolished now in England, Wales, Northern Ireland and here in the Republic of Ireland, due to the breaking up of a generalised crime of "larceny" into specific crimes of burglary, robbery, fraud, theft and related crimes. However "larceny" remains an offence in parts of the United States and in New South Wales in Australia, and involves the taking and carrying away of personal property. I just mention all of this to give you an idea of how the basic laws may be the same across a number of countries and how certain aspects of it are retained or have been amended slightly, as time progressed, in some countries.'

At that point, Aver had become very interested in this aspect of crime and asked what the difference was between that sort of crime and threatening to hit somebody or attacking somebody and causing them harm or injury or even killing them. Mumu explained as simply as she could that the consequences are obviously much more serious, but it is interesting to be aware that, in terms of the law, there is not too much difference between a crime against property and a crime against the person. Crime against property is also considered very, very serious.

Nova then said that she had heard someone on television talking about 'libel' and 'slander', and asked what all that was. Mumu explained that in order to answer that question, they would first have to discuss and understand what it means 'to have a right to your good name'.

'What is your good name? Your good name is your reputation, your standing in life. It is what people think of you. So if somebody says something bad about another person that is untrue, it means that they are attacking the "good name" of that person, trying to give the impression to other people that that person is not a good person or that they are not to be trusted. They are hoping to cause other people to think badly of the person so, the law says, through tradition over many years in lots of countries, that every human being has a right to preserve the integrity of their "good name". Libel arises if you write something bad about somebody that is untrue and slander is if you say it. That is, uttering it, or saying it any way you can say it, in the presence of other people, where you express something about another person which is not just a criticism that you can back up with facts, but something that is untrue about a person that causes them to be seen in a bad light by people based on false statements.'

There was silence for a while as the group seemed to be thinking about the notion of having a right to your good name.

Nova broke the silence by saying, 'You know, Mumu, that is really interesting, and it makes me think about people using social media to spread false and harmful things about their friends and spreading rumours in school. I also wanted to ask you about the time you took us on a tour around the some of the courts. There were so many things to ask after that day, but could you tell us about the differences between all of the courts?'

'Oh yes,' added Lex, 'there was a District Court, a Circuit Court, a High Court, an Appeals Court and a Supreme Court.'

'Thank you for asking about all of that. Yes, I should have really mentioned more details at the beginning but I remember that there was a lot to discuss that day.

'The District Court deals with the lower-value claims or cases, but it also deals with the early stages of criminal cases and orders in relation to Family Law cases. The Circuit Court is the next level up (County Court, they might call it in England, Wales and in Northern Ireland), and that would deal with cases of a value up to a higher amount and then cases over that limit, in terms of cash value or property, would be in the High Court.

'Then there is an Appeals Court, which is a very important and fundamental part of the legal system. An accused person, or someone taking a claim, must have a right of appeal whenever a decision has been made against them. That means that such a person has an opportunity to submit that the decision of the judge in the lower court was wrong. So if a judge in the District Court makes a decision against you, you can appeal it to the next court up – to the Circuit Court, and similarly from the Circuit Court to the High Court, and ultimately to the Appeals Court and the Supreme Court. Before we had an Appeals Court in this country, the Supreme Court was the Court of Final Appeal, but because the Supreme Court became so busy, with a backlog of cases mounting, it is now reserved for cases of a very high importance, such as constitutional cases.'

'Mumu, I heard somebody talking about judges "taking an oath"; what does that mean?' asked Nova.

'When a person is being appointed as a judge they go into the Supreme Court, which as the highest court in the land is where they are "sworn in". They receive a warrant of appointment from the president in this country, but their "swearing in" is the moment that they publicly take that special judicial oath. They swear that they will perform the duties of their office as a judge without "fear or favour"; can you guess what that means?'

There was a long silence, but afterwards Nova came up with a very good answer:

'I think that it means that you make your judgements fairly, without thinking about who the person before you is; that you are not afraid of making a decision against a bad person, just like you were telling us about Lady Justice, when she had the blindfold on, that justice was not going to be intimidated in any way because of somebody being very rich or very powerful; that it was going to be the same justice for everybody.'

'Well done, Nova, that is a very good answer. Yes, it does mean that judges have to be truly independent, and it goes without saying that it could not be otherwise. Of course, judges have to be independent to conduct their very serious work without being intimidated by somebody or without favouring one side against the other. They have to listen to the evidence, listen to the facts and, if there is a jury, sum up and guide the jury, but they have to apply the law and not let their own personal view of what has happened or how the people have behaved come into it.'

'Are there countries where judges might be intimidated so that they could not be truly fair?' asked Aver.

'That is a very relevant question because, sadly, the answer is that sometimes governments, or faulty political systems, or an atmosphere of corruption, create an environment where judicial independence is threatened.'

'Oh no,' was the reaction from Nova. 'What about the people in those countries where they cannot trust the legal system for fairness and depend on the symbols of Lady Justice.'

'I can see that Aver is about to ask me what corruption is, but we have had a busy day, so let us talk about that another time. In the meantime, it would be an important word to ask your parents or teachers about if there is time for discussion.'

Nine

The background to the European Union – misuse of social media – data protection – widening access to justice – the office of ombudsman – human rights

The next time that Mumu met with her group of young people who were interested in finding out about how the law and its processes work, and how they all combine to protect people and provide a vital safeguard to democracy, human rights, fairness and justice, she decided to go to a very quiet park overlooking the sea, where they all sat down on benches close to the fountain with the gentle sound of the water trickling down, which was very conducive to having a reflective chat.

After a few minutes she realised that all had worked very hard during the last number of meetings and she expressed her appreciation to them for maintaining interest in this project, which must have been challenging at times. She suggested that they might have another discussion, and maybe recall some matters already discussed, and then all of them could start thinking about what they had found out, noting any questions they had, as well as thinking about any clarifications which they needed from Mumu.

So Mumu set out a plan: they would sit for some time going through a few more details and then they would go to a cosy café nearby and have a bite to eat.

'Well,' Mumu declared as she opened the conversation and set the ball rolling, 'we did say at the outset of this project that every country has its own legal principles, policies and processes, but what I told you I found interesting was that if it is accepted that we are all aiming for a fair outcome and yet we approach things differently to achieve that, how much do our systems and processes reflect our national traditions and our own way of looking at the world? When we have information about the French system from Verity, we may have more of an understanding about that.'

'Yes,' said Lex, 'I think it will be interesting to see how the judges work on the cases there; as you said, they are involved in investigating things at the early stage.'

'That brings me to another very large subject,' said Mumu. 'You probably all heard a lot on the news recently about something called Brexit and you are probably all wondering why it headlines nearly every day in the news and in the newspapers. Well, I would like to be able to explain it to you succinctly and clearly, but I am sure you will forgive me for not being able to do that in a few words because it is a very complex area, and many people who study this subject are wondering how things have got into such a muddle. You will recall that we discussed the world wars, the First World War (1914–1918) and the Second World War, which ended in 1945 with the most of Europe in devastation – lives, countries, absolutely obliterated and ruined, terrible suffering, bitterness, loss of life and people scarred forever by the experience of a cruel and vicious war that went on for so long from 1939.

'Throughout central Europe at the end of the Second World War people began to consider the benefits of some of the countries in Europe joining together to trade with one another. The idea was that if there could be closer relationships through business and trade, it might keep people engaged with one another, recognising their differences, but also recognising what they had in common, and so there might be less likelihood of conflict between them ever erupting again. So some countries got together with the idea of forming what they described then as the European Economic Community (EEC) and later described as the Common Market. Roughly speaking, the founding states that decided to create this grouping were Germany, Italy, France, the Netherlands, Belgium and Luxembourg. As time went on, the benefits of this co-operation were recognised as being substantial; so in the 1960s the United Kingdom considered joining, and at that time Ireland was struggling economically, and it also considered the benefits. The result was that in 1973 Ireland, Denmark and the United Kingdom joined the European Economic Community. A couple of years after that they held a referendum in the United Kingdom and a substantial majority of people voted to stay in. Unfortunately, as the years progressed, more and more people in the United Kingdom were focusing on the negative sides of the arrangement and thought that they were giving more than they were gaining.

'In June 2016 the British Government held a referendum and 51.89% of the people voted to leave. The results of the referendum were very interesting because in a way it exposed differences of opinion or different experiences within the country. For example, in London the majority of people voted to remain, Scotland voted to remain and so did Northern Ireland. As a result, there are complexities and political problems arising out of all that. Although Northern Ireland, which has had a hard-won international agreement in place for the last twenty years to maintain peace on this island, voted to remain, because it is still part of the United Kingdom it will therefore leave the European Union. This could have serious consequences by creating a border dividing Northern Ireland and the Republic of Ireland which, although it was already legally in place, had eased considerably over the last twenty years from a practical point of view. Indeed, after Brexit there could be border restrictions dividing Northern Ireland and the European Union.'

'Oh dear, that sounds as if things would be moving backwards,' suggested Aver.

'I saw advertisements on British television telling people to start finding out how the new arrangements would affect their everyday life,' added Rex.

'Yes, I saw those,' echoed Lex. 'It looks as if many things would have to change.'

'Well, yes,' said Mumu. 'If we recall what we were discussing about countries having different legal systems but yet, at the same time, having a common denominator in relation to their objectives for justice and peace and fair deals, it seemed reassuring to me to know that all the EU member countries were communicating in relation to many aspects of legal protections. One of the many benefits of the European Union, as we now call it, was that over the last number of years there were many regulations introduced about food, medicines, agriculture, and safety at work, and lots of other areas of our lives that need to be regulated, with strict guidelines for the protection of people against possible abuses.

'One of the legal safeguards was data protection, which is now seen as an essential protection. In a nutshell, it means that all of the information about us in this internet age, which you all take for granted but which did not exist to the same extent before, means that personal information about us – about what we like, what we read, what our choices are, even what our views are about certain political matters – is now available for analysis that various interested people can conduct for financial and/or political gains. By using very complicated algorithms, it is possible to work out a lot about us from the pattern of our likes and dislikes – the things we buy, the areas we show interest in on the internet. They are able to devise what they describe as a "profile" of us, which means that they can assess whether we would be the kind of people who might not only buy a certain thing but even vote in a certain way.

'And there have been many controversies about this hitting the news. One in particular suggested that some people, who had been campaigning in the United Kingdom to leave in the Brexit referendum, had allegedly contacted Facebook with a view to asking them to do an analysis of a certain area where there would be what they call "floating votes". In other words, what could be described as the don't knows or the in-betweeners – people who wouldn't be too sure of exactly what way they feel about something until the eleventh hour when they have to cast their vote. When they had identified these "floating voters", they then asked Facebook to do an advertising campaign pitched towards those people.'

'That is quite scary to me because it was being done without the people knowing what was going on; that would be similar to someone breaking into your house to snoop around and going through all your private belongings and papers,' said Nova.

'Yes, exactly; this is just one small example of what people are beginning to recognise has been going on for some time "under the radar". There have also been many allegations about this kind of research and targeted advertising being done in the United States in order to gain votes during the last presidential election. We might return to this subject later when you have had some time to think about it.

'Let us talk about a good law, data protection, which means that in every European country, and indeed in some other countries outside Europe, there is what we describe as a data protection commissioner set up to operate regulation, through a public office, with laws that limit and protect access to other people's personal information that must be kept private. If somebody is in a relationship with a person that involves them having access to or custody of certain pieces of information, they must apply care and attention to ensuring that it is stored securely.'

'Would that be like a bank that would have a lot of information about a person?' asked Aver.

'Yes, that is right. Perhaps this is a good time to mention that there is another side of access to information. In order to create an open and free society, it was decided many years ago that it was desirable for countries with that objective to have what we describe as Freedom Of Information (FOI) laws, which mean that we have a right to find out what was recorded in connection with government or local authority decisions so that the citizens cannot be "locked out" of decisions that would have an effect on their lives.'

'How does that work?' asked Lex.

'Well, the citizen usually has to pay a small amount of money with their request for a piece of information. Again, there is usually an office of commissioner that oversees this and handles the requests.

'One of the significant advantages that we gained

from being part of the European Union was lots of serious thinking about how we could extend our hard-won rights and freedoms to a larger section of European communities. The result of this was that a European Convention on Human Rights was drawn up, setting out the basic foundations of what we believe people are entitled to in order to preserve their dignity, their freedom, their right to choose in relation to casting a vote, and their right of access to justice, which is a very important part of that – and one that we will discuss today. That convention came into effect in 1953.

'However, objectives are one thing and, in reality for practical reasons, people might not always be able to pursue their rights through the courts. I sometimes use an old expression which goes along these lines: "The law courts of England are as open to every man as the door of the Ritz Hotel." Well now, if we are in an ironic humour we should be able to understand that. In other words, you can say that everybody has a right of access to the courts but, just as the saying goes, not everybody would have the money to go to the Ritz Hotel and walk in, because it is one of the most expensive hotels in London. So, that's a way of hinting at the fact that although countries might say everybody has access to justice, you would need a lot of resources, particularly if you were an individual trying to make a claim against a large organisation if you had a dispute with them, such as, for example, an insurance company or a bank.

'Now, you remember, a few discussions ago we talked about the fact that in France and other continental European countries they have what we describe as inquisitorial or investigative approaches to their court cases, whereas in common law countries we have what is described as an "adversarial" system, meaning that each side contests the evidence of the person against them. We mentioned the role of the barristers, who are pleading the case, presenting submissions, questioning and cross-examining the witnesses for the other side; each side is trying to reduce the credibility of the evidence being given by the opposing side by trying to undermine the creditworthiness or the truthfulness of the people who are giving their evidence in support of their side of the story. As you can imagine, that is a very expensive process. So how would people be able to pursue their claims against a large organisation? Or how could they proceed if the local authority was not giving them the services they required, or if, say, they could not get information about something in the health service that adversely affected their family?

'The answer is that there is help at hand for such circumstances: it is an office called the "office of ombudsman". In many ways we owe the origins and the success of that institution to other European countries, particularly Nordic lands, where Sweden claims credit for being the initiator of that concept. Evidently the king of Sweden, over 200 years ago, came up with this idea when he cogitated about what would happen if the ordinary citizen felt that the administration of public bodies, local authorities, and other designated functions, had fallen below a desirable administrative standard of service to that citizen?

'So, the idea was born of having an ombudsman, which in Nordic languages means a sort of commissioner – a fully independent person to whom the ordinary citizen can refer their complaint without having to incur great expense. I must point out that the word is used in a generic sense – that is, it not male or female – so it does not imply that the office holder is necessarily a man.

'Then over time the concept of ombudsman gained much respect and credibility, not just in relation to government departments or local authorities or health services but, indeed, for different sectors of society and services. Where there is an ombudsman, the citizen can purchase necessary insurance policies or be involved with a financial institution, knowing that if they run into any dispute about a claim, or about something they allege has been done badly by their insurance company or bank, they can refer their case to the appropriate sector ombudsman.'

'That sounds like a very good idea. Do people have to pay for that?' asked Rex.

'No, there is no charge in this part of the world that I know of. So the idea works very well. I recall that you asked me in one of our discussions about what happens about bad policeman. Do you remember? We discussed the awful prospect of somebody who lets the whole organisation down by doing something that is in breach of their standards of service or against their professional disciplinary codes.'

'I asked about that,' said Nova.

'Well, in relation to the police, there may be an organisation called the police complaints board, and in recent years some countries put in place an office of police ombudsman, who can deal with complaints by members of the general public if they feel that a member of the police force has behaved badly or treated them inappropriately. Such an ombudsman would consider the facts of the case rather in the style that I explained to you applies in France and other continental countries, where the judges do a lot of the initial sifting and investigation of the claim, not in an adversarial way but in an inquisitorial way – considering all the circumstances of the case, going through the evidence and using quite wide powers of adjudicating – that is, making a decision and recommendation for a resolution of the dispute.

'Why is it such a good way of resolving disputes, you might ask. Primarily because an ombudsman is not bound by some strictures of the law as a judge would be, therefore the ombudsman can view the complaint through a slightly wider prism with a more equitable approach, having taken into account all of the circumstances of the case. An ombudsman is not strictly bound by precedent, which means that there may not be the same outcome in every complaint, because they can consider the circumstances of the complainant who has referred the case – maybe they were vulnerable in some way; maybe they were not given proper advice before they were sold insurance policy products which turned out to be totally unsuitable for their needs.

'I recall a very good example of this from when I was the Insurance Ombudsman of Ireland! We had a case that we described as *The Titanic Case,* which we recorded in our digest of case histories as a stark example of how trusting people can be unfairly treated. I received a complaint from a woman whose mother had recently died, and when the daughter was going through her mother's papers to sort out her affairs, she came across four additional insurance policy products that had been sold to her mother shortly before she had passed away. When we investigated this matter, it turned out that they were very costly investment-type policies. The policy brochure stated, in quite small print, that these were suitable for long-term investments. When I had spoken to the daughter, she said that her mother had been born on the day of the famous *Titanic* disaster and that she always told people this, so it was highly likely that she would have mentioned it to the insurance company salesman. He had not only sold her four policies that she did not need, but he had sold her policy products that would not be of any value for up to twenty years, so considering her advanced years, which he should have known about, that meant that they were worthless!

'So, just like some of the subjects we have discussed already, what we are seeing emerging over the last few years are new and effective ways of dealing with disputes that aim to widen access to justice and to prevent people from being unable to pursue their rights simply because they do not have the money to pay for a lawyer. Going to court runs the risk of losing a lot of money because if someone loses a case, the judge might make a finding of costs, which means that they would have to pay not only their own legal costs, but those of the organisation against whom they had taken the case.'

The group all said how impressed they were by the sound of the ombudsman system.

'I know that I have mentioned human rights quite a lot in the course of our meetings, and it is important to give you the background to the peoples of the world coming together to agree on setting out the aims of providing for the basic needs of their citizens. We have looked back to the state of the world after two world wars, when there had been a growing recognition that people needed some way of resolving their conflicts through discussion and dialogue. The League of Nations was an international organisation, headquartered in Geneva, Switzerland, created after the First World War to provide a forum for resolving international disputes, but a new international body called the United Nations (UN) came into being in 1945, shortly after the end of the Second World War. The stated purpose of the UN was to bring peace to all nations of the world. After the Second World War, a committee of persons headed by Mrs Eleanor Roosevelt, the wife of US President Franklin D. Roosevelt, wrote a special document which "declares" the rights that everyone in the entire world should have –

called the Universal Declaration of Human Rights. Today there are 192 member states of the UN, all of whom have signed up to the Universal Declaration of Human Rights.

'To the question, "Where do universal rights begin?" Mrs Roosevelt said: "In small places, close to home – so close and so small that they cannot be seen on any maps of the world. Yet they are the world of the individual person; the neighbourhood he lives in; the school or college he attends; the factory, farm or office where he works. Such are the places where every man, woman, and child seeks equal justice, equal opportunity, equal dignity without discrimination. Unless these rights have meaning there, they have little meaning anywhere. Without concerted citizen action to uphold them close to home, we shall look in vain for progress in the larger world."

'This gave rise to what is called the Universal Declaration of Human Rights in 1948 – seventy years ago this year! It is worth reading in full when you get time, really to my mind because of the outright bravery and ambition to get consensus on rights that had been completely ignored and violated during the two world wars.

'A simplified version of the 30 Articles of the Universal Declaration of Human Rights has been created especially for young people, and I have brought along a copy for all of you.'

Mumu gave the pages to Aver to distribute and wondered who would like to read out the words. Both Nova and Lex spoke at the same time so it was agreed that Nova would start and hand over to Lex. They read:

1. We Are All Born Free & Equal. We are all born free. We all have our own thoughts and ideas. We should all be treated in the same way.

2. Don't Discriminate. These rights belong to everybody, whatever our differences.

3. The Right to Life. We all have the right to life, and to live in freedom and safety.

4. No Slavery. Nobody has any right to make us a slave. We cannot make anyone our slave.

5. No Torture. Nobody has any right to hurt us or to torture us.

6. You Have Rights No Matter Where You Go. I am a person just like you!

7. We're All Equal Before the Law. The law is the same for everyone. It must treat us all fairly.

8. Your Human Rights Are Protected by Law. We can all ask for the law to help us when we are not treated fairly.

9. No Unfair Detainment. Nobody has the right to put us in prison without good reason and keep us there, or to send us away from our country.

10. The Right to Trial. If we are put on trial this should be in public. The people who try us should not let anyone tell them what to do.

11. We're Always Innocent Till Proven Guilty. Nobody should be blamed for doing something until it is proven. When people say we did a bad thing we have the right to show it is not true.

12. The Right to Privacy. Nobody should try to harm our good name. Nobody has the right to come into our home, open our letters, or bother us or our family without a good reason.

13. Freedom to Move. We all have the right to go where we want in our own country and to travel as we wish.

14. The Right to Seek a Safe Place to Live. If we are frightened of being badly treated in our own country, we all have the right to run away to another country to be safe.

15. Right to a Nationality. We all have the right to belong to a country.

When they had finished Mumu said, 'I do hope that you can see that many of these matters have come up in our discussions about the law. It will be interesting at some stage to find out if Verity has learnt about this part of history in her school.'

Ten

Breaking the mould: calls for change – dress code modernised – alternative dispute resolution processes (ADRs) – mediation and reconciliation – the orange grove

'We were talking some time ago about the very large proportion of women who are represented in the legal profession both here and in the United Kingdom and, indeed, some other states, and we also spoke about how women have to struggle to get those rights and become successful in that area, up against quite a lot of opposition, as well as particular policies and attitudes that try to resist the advance of women. We also discussed, when we went to look at the courts, the strict code of dress and how people had to be attired in order to have a right of audience in the courts. Do you remember what the judge would say to somebody if they did not have the right shoes, or a waistcoat on if it was a man?'

'Yes,' said Nova, 'I can remember very well.'

'Well, go on, tell us what they were told.'

'He would say,' and she put on a very stern voice when she said this: 'I do not hear you, Mr So and so.'

The group enjoyed her impersonation and Mumu was very glad that everybody was paying attention to information that had been discussed in their many meetings, which at times was very complex and detailed, so it was encouraging to know that some of the anecdotal or story side of some of the information was making an impact.

So Mumu decided to tell them a story about a very well-known lawyer in the Irish courts who has been mentioned already – Mary Robinson, who later went on to become the first female president of Ireland – and her experience with the dress code at the Bar at one stage in her career when she had become senior counsel.

'The senior counsel way of dressing is even more formal. Do you remember I pointed that out to you when we were walking through the corridors of the courts? You saw that they wear a different gown, which is silk, with a straight collar at the back and long open sleeves, and they wear what looks like a man's formal dress-coat with very elaborate buttons on the cuffs, and then a blouse or shirt underneath with a winged collar and the tabs – the little white tabs that are on the front hanging down. At one point Mary Robinson decided that she was going to wear trousers with that outfit because actually trousers look better with the jacket, and the whole ensemble looked very smart. They were not just any old trousers but properly tailored trousers, and she also decided that coming into the Law Library when she was not in court she would wear a very formal, pin-striped suit, which was a jacket and tailored trousers, which looked extremely appropriate.

'Complaints were later made against her and there was a decision made (this was around 1980) to call her before a disciplinary committee on a Saturday. I think I can remember the article on the front page of *The Irish*

Times recounting that an eminent female senior counsel had failed to turn up to a meeting convened to discuss her wearing trousers in court.

'I would not advise everybody to fail to turn up to a disciplinary hearing, but in that context and given the hard work and endeavour that she had put in to becoming an extremely respected and successful lawyer, I think that she had the right to do what she did – and it certainly made a mark! It was a landmark in a way, because then other women could take solace from that and follow her lead.

'Now, that is not to say that lady barristers could turn up in old trousers or crumpled clothes or dress in any way less formally, but it just meant that the trousers themselves were no longer to be completely forbidden, and nowadays, as you noticed when we walked around the courts, there are lots of female barristers walking around either dressed for court wearing their black gown or going about other business without it, in tailored black trouser suits.

'So, I'm sure all of you, at times, when you hear things on the news about politics (and if we accept that politics could be defined as meaning the science of men and women living together), must think it very odd that grown-up people cannot come up with a system to enable them to get on together and, to quote what one of you said, "to share this world together equally and make the most of it".'

'We can either share it or fight about it, and divide up territories and cause endless wars because of boundaries and wars over borders and land.

'While we're at it, we might just introduce a few more big words here – I hope they're not too big – but we might just bring in the word "reconciliation". That means the restoration or the return to friendly relations, for example when you talk about a "process of reconciliation".

'But what happens if the people were not ever friendly, and so what we are trying to do is bring in the other version of that word, which is "reconciling", which is the action of making one view or belief compatible with another. In other words, saying, well, we see these things slightly differently. You, because of your cultural or other background reasons, see this matter in a different light; but can we find a middle ground or a way, for the moment, of working through those differences while not undermining the beliefs of each side?

'I would be very interested to hear your ideas about this, and perhaps we can discuss those when we are having our meal later.

'Okay, let us summarise a few things and cheer ourselves up. We have fundamental rules in society; and we know that we pay taxes, that are taken out of our wages and our salaries, to pay for hospitals, schools, parks, libraries, the police force, the defence forces, museums, art galleries, lighting in the streets, and lots and lots of other things; and we know that, from time to time, we might be a bit unhappy with the people who are making the rules and we might think that the rules are unfair or ineffective. So we know that there are now opportunities for us in a democratic society to make our views known through the democratic process of free elections, and that all eligible people have a vote and that they can make their voices heard. We know that there are many people who would read or hear this and say, "Well, no one is listening to me" or "Our voices are not heard", but let us just say that there are processes available; and we must – and good politicians should always – make sure that the voices of those who are less able to express themselves, or who do not have access to representatives to the same degree as others, are given an opportunity for their concerns to be addressed.

'We also said that, from time to time, all sensible people when reviewing rules and regulations must ask themselves if those rules are doing what they were supposed to be doing or have they outlived the purpose for which they were drawn up in the first instance? Or do we need to revise them and redraft them? We have also said that now, because society is advancing in some respects, we are finding more adventurous ways of doing things with regard to disputes and conflict. This is called the development of Alternative Dispute Resolution processes, or ADRs for short.

'In some countries with common law jurisdictions (such as Ireland and Britain and others), there are legal processes that are described as the adversarial system. That means that when you go to court, because you have to prove that the other side is wrong in order to prove that you are right, you have to be very aggressive sometimes, and you try to find ways of getting the judge or the jury, if there is one, to think that the person against you cannot be relied upon to be believed. Can I just ask you all to think for a moment: What do you think would be the inevitable outcome of that process?'

There was silence for a moment, then Aver suddenly looked up and said, 'I imagine that if you go through that process, where you are trying to contest some matter against another person and you have to be aggressive, or your lawyers have to be aggressive on your behalf – that after such an experience you would never, ever do business with those people again or indeed have a friendly personal relationship.'

'Oh yes; I was thinking that,' chimed Nova.

'Well done, Aver,' said Mumu. 'That is a very good suggestion and that is exactly the point. And this is why the concept of an ombudsman really started in other countries where they do not have an adversarial system.

The ombudsman idea, as I have said, developed as an alternative way of solving problems between people who have disputes, challenges or complaints with service-providers or institutions. The ombudsman is like a referee. The person in the job must be wholly trusted to act fairly and not take sides, which of course applies to a judge as well. The person must be entirely independent, not involved with, or dependent upon, either "side of the fence". The ombudsman will look at the case and may investigate the disagreement. If people agree to use the ombudsman then they must tell all the truth and let the ombudsman find out all the facts. Then, when the ombudsman has looked at all the facts, she or he makes a decision, called an adjudication, as opposed to a judgement in a court. Of course, the courts are always superior to any other systems for dispute resolution, including the ombudsman or mediation.'

'What does mediation mean?' asked Nova.

'Mediation is a very interesting way of resolving a dispute. It means getting both sides, both of the people (in formal language we refer to them as the "parties") who are in the dispute, to come together and sit down at a table to talk about how their dispute started. It is very helpful, by the way, if that table is a round one, so that there is no sense of them being far away from each other or "on different sides". Both sides need to have a sense of being part of the same circle, where in a safe environment they present their versions of the story, through which they might recognise what has caused the disagreement. The whole purpose is for each side to be able to see the weakness in what they are claiming and the strength of what the other person is saying, and perhaps recognise some options that might bring them to a resolution. One might say: "Look, you have asked me for all of this and I am going to see if I can give you a little bit of that. But I need you in return to give me something." So, the mediator must be impartial and not favour one side over the other. This person needs to be, first of all, a good listener and needs to be very patient because a mediator is a person who helps the people who are disagreeing to recognise the need to find their own solutions. The mediator must resist what is a very tempting, instinctive urge to tell them what they should be doing or advise them, because a mediator is not a judge and is not a lawyer advising the people who are in dispute, but is there to assist them in communicating with each other and, in so doing, to try and construct some form of an agreement which will address some of the needs of the disputants.

'It is not easy, I must say. It is a very difficult and complex job, but it is a very valuable process which requires not only a good mediator who is skilled and experienced in the area, but also fundamentally the good will of the parties, the people who are in dispute. They need to be coming together with an intention in their minds of trying to make the best of it and hoping to make some kind of a settlement. If they come to mediation with their minds set against it and very hostile, then there is little opportunity for breaking that impasse.

'That's a French word – impasse – that I have used there, and it is a very useful word. It means that people come to a position of loggerheads and they cannot get beyond it. You might look it up and you might mention it to Verity and ask her interpretation of it. Most of what we are discussing is a little bit gloomy some of the time, so let me tell you a story that might be of interest, and maybe a source of inspiration.

'There were two villages close together, divided by a beautiful sun-drenched orange grove that produced magnificent big luscious oranges. The people in the villages had been arguing about who owned the land and the orange trees. That dispute had been simmering for years and it caused great hostility, suspicion and aggression between the two neighbouring communities. Each village accused the other of taking more than they should. Each village claimed that they owned the orange grove and wanted to fence it off.

'So we had here what would normally be described as territorial wars, fighting over territory, fighting over land, fighting over resources – which is not unusual in this world that we live in. Families that should have friendly relations were not talking to one another, and the youngsters did not play together, so there was a very bad feeling of aggression and suspicion simmering even among the children and young people.

'At the suggestion of one of the more senior members of the community, the villagers decided that they should approach the process of mediation and engage with it in a positive frame of mind. They also decided to try this before going to fight their claims in court – and believe me, in this story, which is true, they were all about to go to court because anger had become very entrenched.

'So what happened?

'Well, the mediator met the villagers all together in the largest local hall and explained that she was there to help them find their own solutions. She set out and described very clearly what the mediator's role would be, so that nobody was in any doubt about her independence and the role that she played and that she was not there to suggest a settlement or to impose a resolution on anybody, or to make a judgement about the merits of the case.

'So the mediator said that she would meet them in a nearby town, not their towns, the following week, because it was important to be on neutral ground. First of all, she said she would welcome the chance to have a tour of the two individual villages and the famous orange grove.

'A person from each village was appointed by the villagers to act as a guide and as the official spokesperson. As they walked around the village that was closer to the main road, the mediator asked about the work activities of the villagers. It is worth mentioning at this time that the mediator's work had already begun. Why, you might ask. The answer is because she would be very closely observed by each side, who were suspicious, who were at a heightened stage of aggression and agitation, and who would be looking to see if she was giving in any way more time or attention to one side of the story than the other.

'So, having asked about the work activity of the respective villagers, she noticed some long warehouses with delivery vans outside in one of them. It turned out that this village specialised in making a very well-known orange juice and smoothie product that was sold in the best shops and restaurants throughout their country.

'Then the mediator was brought through the beautiful orange grove to the neighbouring village that was in a small valley with grain growing on gently sloping fields. The first thing she noticed was the smaller buildings and, as she went closer, she was surrounded by the most beautiful smell coming from several bakeries. It turned out that these villagers were famous for making the most beautiful Madeira cakes. When she asked about the magic ingredient, she was told that the thick rich peel from the oranges was grated liberally into the cake mixture.

'When the people sat down to try to resolve this dispute that was causing so much upset and broken friendships, the mediator asked each side to explain why they depended on the orange grove and a spokesperson from each village explained how they used the abundant oranges. The mediator asked the villager who made the juices what they did with the peel and he said they threw it out. When it was the time of the other villager to give their side of the argument, the mediator quietly enquired what the bakers did with the zest, the pips and the fruit of the oranges after they had used the peels. They were thrown out.

'When each side had told their version of the history of the local land ownership and submitted their claim that they should have ownership of all of the orange grove, the mediator suggested that each side go to their own rooms for a bit of a break and take time to reflect.

'When they were sitting down with all their anger expelled, they had started to think a bit about what had been said. And, after a while, each side remembered the answers to the mediator's questions given both by them and the other side. "We only need the juice and they only need the peel or the rind," said one. Both communities could have thriving businesses if they agreed to share the orange grove, and they could all become famous for the produce from one small piece of land. The representative from the baker village came out to find the mediator, and as he was walking down the hall the representative and spokesperson from the juice village was coming in the other direction. They knocked on the door and they told the mediator that they would like to talk again.

'The mediation ended with an agreement and a handshake. They agreed to have joint ownership of the land and the orange grove because each side saw that there were benefits in co-operating and joining forces to help all to use their resources wisely. Each side needed the orange grove for different reasons, so they had joint interests in looking after the rich resource which was on their doorstep. With all of the arguing and wariness and suspicion removed, they were free to be more productive and celebrate the successes of the villages together.

'It was necessary after this for their lawyers to meet and to draw up formal headings of an agreement reflecting the discussions they had had with the mediator, detailing matters such as quantity and transport and insurance of the orange grove and the harvesting and storage at various stages of production. Then these operating details had to be agreed, but they were details which the villagers were realistically aware of, and they knew that if the smaller details were fully agreed there would be less likelihood of any further disruption to their production lines or indeed any further disruptions to their relationships.

'We are talking here about what are termed joint interests; we are not talking about people coming in and fighting about their rights, but instead actually recognising and acknowledging that there were, in the set of circumstances involved, joint interests – where one side's interests overlapped with the other's and where, with a bit of positive thinking and objective analysis, they could find a way of resolving the dispute to their mutual gains.'

Eleven

The processes of mediation and arbitration – Legal Aid – law reform

Mumu looked at her diary and realised it would soon be time to have another meeting with her group of curious young people, whom she had come to refer to as 'learners' – a word she had heard used in this way in South Africa. She had been taken by the use and application of the word in relation to schoolchildren and university students and thought it compared so well to the word 'student', which implies that one is doing the job of studying, whereas 'learners' seemed to have a sense to it of those who were interested and inspired to take the information that they were encountering.

She could see through their questions that there were many things that were quite complex for their young minds to understand, but, at the same time, she recognised a hunger there and an interest in more information and in greater understanding of how processes worked and how they benefitted people. Sometimes she was quite taken aback by the simplicity of their questions and it meant that she had to be alert in keeping the information that she was providing steady, focused and at a level that could anticipate the understanding and the interests of the young people.

They were due to meet again soon, and Mumu began to look over the subjects that she had covered and wondered if it was time to let the learners begin to engage in their dialogue with their pen-pal Verity, who would eagerly participate in the project from France, where she had started her legal studies. However, Mumu thought perhaps it was time to reflect on, or go back and clarify, some of the matters that she had covered, and decided that for the next meeting she might concentrate a little on processes and remind everyone about the everyday threats of bullying. She would try to be guided by the level of interest from the group.

She suggested that she would make up a picnic and that they might travel outside Dublin to an amenity in the mountains of County Wicklow near a beautiful waterfall. The drive was not too long but it provided an opportunity for everyone to talk a little bit about their impressions so far.

She collected Nova and Aver and picked up Lex and Rex on the way. As they drove towards the waterfall at Powerscourt, where there were lots of tables and benches at which they could sit down and relax and enjoy their picnic, with the sound of the waterfall in the background, she began by going back to the subject of mediation.

'Do you remember when we talked about using mediation as a way of resolving a dispute that had arisen between the different communities living beside an abundant orange grove?' she asked.

All the learners agreed that the story of resolving the dispute about the orange grove through mediation was very interesting.

'Now, let's just talk a little bit about how that process works. In the story that I described to you it may have come across as quite easy, so I do not want to leave you with the impression that acting as a mediator or a facilitator between people who are in a dispute is in any respect easy. In fact, it is one of the most complex and complicated areas of work. It is true to say that the process itself should be simple, but the job of ensuring that it is kept simple may be extremely difficult.

'A mediator is an independent third party, a person who is not involved in any way in the dispute. If it is a public dispute like the one we discussed about the orange grove, then the people in dispute may approach a solicitor or lawyer, depending on which country they live in, with a view to going to court, and the lawyer may, depending on the country, be legally bound to advise them to undertake a mediation process before going down the court route, and so the solicitors or lawyers will know of mediators available for that kind of work and perhaps put forward two or three names to see if they can agree on one.

'Having agreed on a mediator, the lawyers will tell the people in the dispute that they have selected someone in whom they could place trust and whom they could recommend. In the case of a public dispute like the orange grove, where lots of people had an interest in the outcome because there were so many people involved – we refer to those as "stakeholders": all the villagers and townspeople and the people working in the orange juice and bakery factories – from a practical point of view, they could not all come together to sit around the same table.

'In the case of multi-party disputes, where many party disputants are involved, they nominate someone to speak as their representative, who can then come back to them and report on progress. That is what happened in the orange grove case, because the mediator met the guides or the representatives of each side, as there were two main disputing sides in that particular dispute.

'But what if it is just a dispute between two individuals – two people who are doing business together; a person who is supplying goods and a person who is buying them from that person; or a person who has a contract to carry out certain services?

'Well, when a dispute arises the first instinct, particularly in a country like Ireland, is for people to automatically think of consulting their solicitor about going to court to take a claim to get compensation, or to get the person who has undertaken to do something for them to actually do it, as they had initially promised under the contract.

'So, in this country – and increasingly in many other countries in this part of the world – there is a duty upon solicitors to explain to the people who are their clients that mediation is very cost-effective and simple and should not cost anything in the region of what it would cost to go to court to resolve such disputes.

'Then there would be the question of selecting a mediator – and sometimes there can be problems with that because of the position of the two parties – but ultimately they agree on a mediator who is requested to take the case. At that stage, the mediator has to make a decision as to whether they are suited to do the work, and before making that decision they need to know some facts in confidence about the case, in order to be sure that they have not got what is called a "conflict of interest".

'Can you imagine what that means?'

The group of learners was quite enthusiastic about that, and it did not prove in any way challenging to them. They understood that if somebody had any kind of an interest in the dispute, or if they knew some of the people, then that would create a conflict and they could not be independent.

'Once the mediator has accepted the task of trying to facilitate the dispute, they then meet the parties and, depending on the preferred approach of the mediator, they sit down with both sides of the dispute to begin with and describe the process and their role. They make it very clear that they are not there to make a decision or to make a judgement in any way, and most importantly that they are not there to advise the parties on any legal matters, because each side has their own lawyer to do that.

'There will be an "agreement to mediate", which is a formal legal document in which both sides agree on certain terms which are part of the mediation process, such as that the mediation process is private and confidential and that anything said in the course of the mediation, or any admissions that are made by either side, cannot then be used in a court of law if the mediation fails to produce a resolution at the end.

'Usually each side agrees that they will both be equally responsible for paying the mediator, and that if one side does not pay then the other side will be responsible for the full amount. The mediator will have to very carefully gauge, using great sensitivity, as he or she goes along, whether the parties have had enough time talking together, whether they have had enough time talking privately, whether they need to be left on their own with their solicitor to reflect on what has been said and hold a mirror up to the strengths and weaknesses of each side of the dispute, recognising the weaknesses in their own arguments perhaps, while recognising the strength in the arguments of the other side.

'The mediator will have to time the meetings so that the parties do not get too tired, and will need to know when it is important to let them break for a cup of coffee or perhaps send them off for a meal or to go and stretch their legs in the fresh air. It is always very beneficial if the location of the mediation can be near some open space or even a park, where the parties can go off and get some fresh air and have time to think.

'It is true to say that one of the great powers of mediation is that it is private and confidential, and it gives people an opportunity of speaking freely about the dispute in question. It is also a voluntary process so people should not be forced to go into mediation. Anybody who works in that area will tell you very honestly that it would not work if people felt that they were there through any kind of compulsion.

'Having said that, the trend in this part of the world, and our next-door neighbour's, is to do everything to encourage people in a dispute to go to mediation, and so it has been considered appropriate that people who showed reluctance to make an attempt to go into some form of negotiation or dispute resolution process before going to court would be penalised; that is to say, they would be punished by the judge in that the costs of the action would be awarded against them unless they can persuade the judge that the case was not one suitable for such a settlement.

'Now, let me explain that to you. When you go to court everybody has to be paid and the costs are huge amounts of money, so if you win your case, usually the costs follow that and you will be paid your costs by the person who has brought you through the courts by not admitting or acknowledging that your claim was valid. In some circumstances, even in cases where one side has won, if that is a public body which has been using taxpayers' money, the courts have taken the view that they should pay towards the costs because they should not have been reckless by refusing to go to mediation; they should have recognised that it was a much cheaper way of resolving the dispute and given it a go.

'So although we say that it is voluntary because, under the general principles of our legal system, every citizen has a right to justice in an open court and has the right to have their dispute or their trial heard in court, it is true to say that the trend is towards encouraging people to try mediation before going to court.'

'What sort of a person makes a good mediator, Mumu?'

'There is specific training for people, at various academic levels, about understanding the process and how to apply it in different types of dispute, so people can study the subject and get practical training, but really it has a lot to do with the personality of the person involved. What do you think would be one of the main ingredients?'

There was a quite a silence, and then Nova looked around and said:

'Well, I think the person would need a very good understanding of how people find it difficult to express themselves and tell the story of their dispute.'

'That's a very good suggestion, and to achieve that they need to be good listeners; listening is one of the most important skills for a good conflict resolver. A person who is involved in helping people to find a solution to their own dispute needs to be hearing what the people on each side are saying, in order to understand at what stage it would be appropriate to perhaps put them back together in the same room again or to split them up and put them into separate meetings. And she or he needs to assess, at all times, how each side is responding to the other's points and if they are coming to the stage, as the people did in the case of the orange grove, where they are recognising that their needs are met at one point along the line by the needs of the other side – that there is an overlap.

'There is some jargon used in relation to this subject, which is the kind of language that is used in some mediation textbooks and training, and which I would generally discourage, but there is one catchy little acronym – those are the first initials of the words – which I will introduce you to. It is called the "ZOPA" – "the zone of potential agreement", and we should always have our mind on alert to recognise this as the details of the dispute unfold.

'So, looking at our example of the orange grove, the mediator recognised, at some stage, that perhaps there was an area of possible agreement. The mediator then has to be very discreet, not in any way forcing or expressing a view but hoping to coax the people involved into gradually coming to recognise for themselves that there is an area through which they could find a resolution of the dispute, from which all involved would benefit.

'Over the last number of years, we have come to talk of Alternative Dispute Resolution processes (ADRs), and people refer to this as being one of the big stepping stones in the last twenty years because we have come to value the need for exploring other ways of resolving a dispute than going straight down the courtroom route, which – as I have explained – is adversarial here in the common law system, and leaves everyone badly bruised after the fight.

'Do you remember we discussed the adversarial system? When I told you that that was how we operate in this part of the world – that we have to knock down or discredit the other side in order to prove that our claim or case is correct. This is where it is going to be very interesting to hear what Verity says, because in the inquisitorial system, as we call it – meaning roughly the countries of mainland Europe, which do not have the adversarial system – things are slightly different. It will be good to hear what Verity's understanding is on the subject of how they find their way towards the adjudication of a case without each side having to go into battle, as it were, and do down the other side.

'Of the ADRs that are around at the moment, there is also the ombudsman system that I explained to you. Before all of that is arbitration – said to be one of the oldest forms of alternative dispute resolution, whose use can be traced back many hundreds of years. Arbitration is a process whereby the parties agree to refer their disputes for resolution to an independent third party known as an arbitrator.'

'Oh, is that not like a mediator, Mumu?'

'Well, from what I have just said you are very wise to draw that conclusion, but there is a substantial difference. The arbitrator works to rules agreed between the parties with regard to the form of arbitration that is laid down by the applicable Arbitration Acts, but one of the main differences is that the arbitrator is usually an expert in the subject matter of the dispute, because arbitration is similar to court litigation, in that it usually involves pleadings and a full hearing based on the law of evidence applicable to court proceedings.

'The major advantage to the people participating in this is that it is a confidential and private process, and that the parties involved can decide where and when they have the arbitration. They are not dependent on moving through slow court lists or processes and they can agree to the choice of arbitrator. If they do not agree, the person is appointed by an institution agreed by the parties for that purpose, and the mechanism is usually set out in an arbitration clause in any commercial agreement.

'That it is all very similar to the court process. An arbitrator's award, as it is called, is final and binding, and really there is no appeal against it. A party may, however, apply to set aside an arbitrator's award in some circumstances, but this very rarely occurs.'

They had arrived at that stage at the gates of the Powerscourt Estate with its wonderful waterfall, and drove through, taking in the view and looking out for nice spots where they could stop to have their picnic. When they had stopped and put their basket on a table and set out their picnic, Mumu decided that, having spoken about the huge costs of going through the courts, she should tell the group that everybody in a civilised and democratic society had a right of access to justice and to the courts, and that there is a concept called Legal Aid, whereby help is provided, by the State, if a person cannot afford to pay a solicitor privately.

'Legal Aid provides legal advice and representation in court in certain circumstances, depending on the type of claim and on the ability of the people involved to pay. Such considerations as their income, what they own and what their personal circumstances are would all be taken into consideration.

'So here in this country, Northern Ireland, England and Wales, and in Scotland, there is help for people who are not in a position to pay for legal representation. It is quite a complicated process and it is also quite controversial because it costs the State a lot of money, but there is a Legal Aid Board to which people may apply for help when they need it.

'I would also like to mention,' said Mumu, 'the question of how laws arrive, as it were. I think I mentioned to you briefly before that some laws were there for hundreds and hundreds of years. Some have evolved over time, such as in the "snail in the bottle" case. Some have been repealed, meaning that they have been brought up to date or altered in some way. And then there are instances where a government might have come into power on the basis that they would carry out certain reforms and certain new legislation, or propose new legislation which would then be debated in parliament. I think we discussed this before.

'And then there might be an individual politician, either in the government or in the opposition parties, who might have some idea of a particular area of law that needs to be introduced or changed, and they might introduce a private member's bill. A bill just means draft legislation proposed to parliament, and that, of course, would be debated before it would stand any chance of ever becoming law. Such a piece of legislation would be subject to all sorts of criticism and review and possible challenge, and then eventually, if it did receive common support and consensus, it would be brought into law.

'It is also important to bear in mind that the law is continuously under review in this country and the United Kingdom. There is a special commission, a Law Reform Commission, which is an independent, objective and expert review group that is there to make recommendations for law reform and to make current law accessible for all.

'These Law Reform Commissions in this part of the world all agree that, to be successful, law reform must be an inclusive process, and so they encourage people – citizens of the State – to become involved in the process of law reform by contacting them with suggestions or making comments on current reports that they bring out from time to time. They may also issue papers or encourage consultation on certain issues. In that way citizens have a means of contributing to debates about the reform of the law. It is an empowering and important process, and one which should be greatly cherished.'

Twelve

Data protection – social media and politics – the Nobel Prize – the voices of poets in sharing wisdom

'I would like now like to return to a subject that we touched on the other day – and let me tell you how I came to think about it again today. Early this morning, on the radio, I heard reference to a poet called Seamus Heaney. He was from Northern Ireland and a very famous international poet by the time he died, which was in 2013. So we are celebrating five years of his death this very month. There has been an exhibition put in place to mark the five years since his death and I hope that we can go and visit that together at some stage.

'But back to the connection between the radio programme about the poet this morning and talking to you. They played a recording of his voice in an interview from some time back, in which, among other things, he was saying that "we all live on the conveyor belt of our generation". That made me think of all of you and the fact that you are on a different conveyor belt, and that your conveyor belt in many respects is, in my view, dominated by technology and social media. Hopefully, in the future your lives will not be as controlled by social media as they are now. It will be for your generation to balance that relationship.

'We are living through a very dramatic period of our history because in the course of the last year or so a number of major things have happened politically. First of all, there was an election in America for a new president, and President Donald Trump was elected two years ago; and also in 2016, there was a referendum held in the United Kingdom as to whether they would remain in the European Union, and the result of that referendum was to leave, even though it was not by a large majority. This has given rise to many challenges and difficulties in trying to work out how the United Kingdom will actually exit from the relationship it had been in for so many years – not only from an economic and trade point of view, but also from all the legal and regulatory connections that have been drawn up and sewn into a connecting tapestry of working relationships over the last forty years or so.

'There has recently been quite a lot of concern expressed about the role that social media platforms, such as Facebook, have had on the way people have voted, and suggestions have been made that this amounts to a major challenge to democracy as we know it. Stories have emerged about companies who carried out research having managed to gain access to data which was provided by Facebook on Facebook account holders.

'There have been suggestions in the United States that some such companies harvested personal data. Yes, "harvested" is the word that they use, and in many ways it is very descriptive. They take information that is part of somebody's personal data and gather it together to form a view of what kind of person I am – my profile, as it is called. They are able to assess what kind of person

I am by the subjects that I am interested in, where I like to travel, what books and articles I read and what films I like. Ultimately they form a decision that I am a "such and such" type of person and therefore I'm likely to vote in a certain way or be a "middle ground person" or I am a "don't know". That means that if they are campaigning for a referendum or for a presidential or governmental election, they know a lot about where to pitch their advertising, and where to spend more of their campaign budget and time making their case attractive to the people they think might vote for them.

'Now, if all of these stories that we are hearing are true, and if companies like Facebook are providing data about individuals to companies who want to use that information to find out where they should concentrate their work or where they should target their campaign to get people who would be amenable to their persuasion to vote for whatever it was they wanted them to vote for, then what are the implications of all this?

'Really, if we talk about this further and we consider the great sums of money involved here, where information that is personal and private about me becomes the subject of a bargain between people who are using that information for certain gains, that is called bullying on a grand scale. Let us use the word openly. These people are engaged in exploitation and bullying.

'So, for example, this morning there was news coming out that a report in the United Kingdom has shown that social media is "the most significant factor" driving harassment and intimidation of political candidates. It was reported that some Members of Parliament are warning about the extent of interference in elections, claiming that the spread of fake news and data manipulation is throwing the country into a democratic crisis. They are calling for tougher regulation on social media corporations. It has been quoted in the newspapers today that some are saying that the English public is being increasingly manipulated by campaigns and disinformation and fake news in social media. All of this information is said to come from a parliamentary enquiry that was being conducted into the implications of all of this.

'I mention this to you because you are now on "the conveyor belt" of this technology. You are growing up in an era where you think of all of these social media platforms as being "the norm" in your way of life, and so it is very important that your generation takes a very objective, hard, cold view of these developments. You must understand what the dangers and risks are so that any engagement that you have with these social media platforms is an informed one, and that you know what the implications are and what the threats are, both to your privacy and to your precious democracy and freedom.

'Some of the reports say that there is a relentless campaign aimed at the fears and prejudices of certain kinds of people in order to influence their voting plans. So, it looks as if it is time for real action, and I just hope that people are going to be strong in taking a stand and that the general public is going to have time to fully digest what the implications are now, in the medium term, and long term, if this trend is not stopped with proper regulation and legislation.

'We need those valuable "checks and balances"; we need ways of ensuring that our privacy and our rights to our own self-determination are not taken away by people who are really attempting to hold power through influence and bully the electorate into voting for them when they have obtained information about these people through illicit means.

'Now, you might say to me: Mumu, we see it every

day when we are driving to school when there is either a local election or a general election – people put posters up, they go door-to-door with their campaign supporters and volunteers, knocking on doors saying "Please vote for me", big posters go up saying " Vote for the XYZ party".'

'Or,' said Nova, 'the Raving Loony Party.'

Aver laughed.

'Yes, Nova, you are quite right, people do that. People do go to voters' doors, people do go on radio and television and have their interviews. But what's the difference?'

'We can see and hear them,' suggested Lex.

'Yes, one of the main differences is that when the candidates are running in an election or being proposed to be president or are proposing or objecting to the suggestions of a referendum, they are identified. Also, they all have an equal amount of time to speak and an equal amount of time to represent their views, on radio and television, which is very carefully balanced – and has to be, because all of the actions coming up to any significant election are overseen by an Electoral Commission to ensure that the information that is being put out is fair, balanced and accurate.

'Also, I would add that there are other differences, in that if a politician goes to somebody's door to ask for a vote, they see that person living in a certain place and the person comes out to the door if they wish to speak to them or ask them a question or express a view, and they are free to do so. The politician on the doorstep, hoping for a vote, may make certain promises or undertakings. They may be standing for a political party which has particular views and policies. Those policies are generally transparent and known, and the person on the other side of the door, the potential voter, may ask questions or say that they disagree with certain aspects of that party or, indeed, close the door abruptly and tell them to go away – that they think they are hopeless. So people have an opportunity of speaking back. They have an opportunity of demonstrating their right to say no, or to agree to vote for the person there and then.

'There is a distinct difference between that and people being able to secretly find out your social profile so that they can specifically target you in an advertising campaign that has somehow concluded that you are the sort of person who would be amenable to a certain kind of influence or persuasion.

'In fact, I think if we sat down and thought about that for too long, and what the long-term implications of that could be if it went unchecked, we would become very upset and depressed, because it paints a very bleak picture.'

Mumu looked at the group, who were depending on her for so much information. She became acutely aware of the fact that she was in some respects insinuating some of her concerns and prejudices into the group's experiences of finding out about aspects of law and its role in the way we organise society, and so she felt compelled to qualify some of what she had been saying.

'Just before we move on from where I acknowledged that I had painted a bleak picture, I need to expand a little. We have been touching on the subject of the loss control over our private information and the way that such information could be put to improper use, and I must make you aware, in case you get the impression that these are just my views and concerns, that there are many professional commentators, from a range of disciplines and perspectives, who raise awareness about these matters through their research and writing. I would mention a well-respected academic based in the United States, who has written extensively on these subjects. Sherry Turkle is professor of the Social Studies of Science and Technology at the Massachusetts Institute of Technology (MIT). Her area of interest and research looks at how computers are not tools so much as part of our social and psychological lives, and so she focuses on the psychology of human relationships with technology, particularly in the realm of how people relate to one another.

'Sherry Turkle has written several books, one called Alone Together, another called Life on the Screen, and she has given many TED talks. I don't know if you have ever watched any of those, but they are very interesting talks given by people of knowledge and experience about subjects that they wish to communicate. I saw one talk she gave in the TED series that was called Connected, But Alone, which is one of the themes that she studies on a continuing basis. She examines how a flight from conversation undermines our relationships, creativity and productivity, and why reclaiming face-to-face conversation can help us regain lost ground. In a nutshell, she will say that we live in a technological universe in which we are always communicating and yet we have somehow sacrificed conversation for mere connection. Some of her observations centre on the idea that developing technology seems to promise closeness. She will say that sometimes it delivers on that, but that much of our modern life leaves us less connected with people and more connected with simulations of them. She has also spent a lot of time discussing the problems that arise when children pose as adults online and, in many respects, we know that these problems are presenting difficulties in our world every day. This is a subject I think that we should return to again. I would be very interested in hearing your ideas about this and all the related topics that specialists like Sherry Turkle have made the centre of their research and writing.

'Now I am talking about very gloomy things, so let me for a moment, before we leave this beautiful place, tell you a little bit more about Seamus Heaney, and maybe we could just cheer ourselves a little? I don't know if you know of him from school or if you are aware him, but he won the Nobel Prize for Literature, which is a very significant award made every year by the Swedish Academy to authors for outstanding contributions in the field of literature. In fact, you might mention this to Verity because the first Nobel Prize for Literature was awarded in 1901 to a person called Sully Prudhomme. That was a pseudonym. Do you know what a pseudonym is?'

'No, Mumu, what's a pseudonym?'

'It is an assumed name. Somebody might change their name for writing purposes or if they were an actor they might decide to call themselves something else. But Sully Prudhomme was the pseudonym of René François Armand. So his full name was René François Armand Prudhomme, but he called himself Sully! We shall never know why.

'So, back to Seamus Heaney, who was born in 1939, just at the outbreak of the Second World War, at a family farmhouse in Northern Ireland, and he was the first of nine.

'You should look him up and find out a little bit more about him and about his varied career. Everybody has their favourite poem of Heaney's, but one of the poems that always sticks in my mind is one about his relationship with his mother, because it gives the reader a little insight into how close he was to her and how seriously he took his role as the eldest of a family of nine children.

'Can you just imagine for a moment in those days, when incomes would have been very low in the countryside, nine children on a farm – how difficult it would have been to feed all the children, just in terms of being able to find the resources to do so? But also imagine preparing a meal for eleven people every day, including the parents.

'This is the poem, and it is about helping his mother peel the potatoes in readiness for a meal. All of the other family members have gone to church and so the poem is called 'When All the Others Were Away at Mass'.

'When all the others were away at Mass
I was all hers as we peeled potatoes.
They broke the silence, let fall one by one.
Like solder weeping off the soldering iron:
Cold comforts set between us, things to share
Gleaming in a bucket of clean water.
And again let fall. Little pleasant splashes
From each other's work would bring us to our senses …

'That's all I'm going to give you of that poem. There is another verse but it is a little bit sad because it is about the time that his mother was dying. I will not read that today, so let us keep cheerful enjoying our sandwiches.

'During the time of what seemed like unending conflict between the communities in Northern Ireland, Seamus Heaney spoke a few short words that I often quote, to sum up how he and many people felt: "The voice of reason has grown hoarse."

'Do those words make sense to you?'

'Yes.' Nova was the first to reply in what was a chorus of agreement.

'I can even see the image he is creating of all the people calling out for the communities to stop fighting,' said Rex.

'Would that be about reconciliation?' asked Lex, and the others all answered for Mumu.

Thirteen

In search of a fair deal – the reasonable view – the man on the Clapham omnibus – anti-bullying protections

As they left the beautiful surroundings of the Powerscourt waterfall, Mumu had the impression that her trusty band of learners might have reached a point of overload. Perhaps she had given them quite a lot of information to digest over the course of the previous few weeks, so she decided to put the question to them.

'I'm a little bit concerned that perhaps I have given you too much detail and we have gone into too many subjects. What do you feel about our project at this stage?' she said.

'Oh no,' said Aver. 'This is all very interesting, Mumu, and we appreciate everything that you have told us. The only thing we are concerned about is that we need to try and work on the information and decide on our own questions, and then put them into different subject headings, give them to Nova, who will put them in order into sections for Verity in France, and then wait for her replies.

'So, what we have done so far is to send her two sections.'

'Oh,' said Mumu, 'I'm very pleased. I was not up to date on that.'

'Yes, we asked her about symbols of justice outside the courts in France. We asked her about the role of the lawyers and how the responsibilities were split. You remember, Mumu, you told us about the distinction, here in Ireland and the UK, between the lawyers who are solicitors, the people to whom the general public can go directly, and the lawyers who are barristers, whom the general public cannot approach directly but have to hire through a solicitor. Well, we asked her about that area and we also asked about what people wear in the courts in France.'

'Yes,' said Rex, piping up from the back of the car. 'We also decided to ask her if they have faith in the judiciary and the legal system in France and what they think about their police force.'

'Good, that's progress. So, we shall await with interest the news from France.'

'Well, just in case you were left with the impression that law was a stuffy and very boring area – and I do hope you have not been left with that impression – I would like to remind you that there are times when judges can display a certain sense of irony and maybe even a little humour. There has always been this quest for finding a level of fairness, a way of defining what people might regard as reasonable.

'I personally believe,' said Mumu, 'that all people are looking for in life could be summarised as "a fair deal". So, in the quest for assessing what the ordinary person in the street would think about disputes, there was an attempt to try and find a way of objectifying that by imagining what the so-called reasonable person would think about something – how they would feel about outcomes being fair or unfair, or acceptable or unacceptable. And so, way back in time, the phrase came up in a case about an imaginary person – "the man on the Clapham omnibus". Now let us begin at the beginning. Clapham is a suburb in London and an omnibus is an old-fashioned word for a bus, and in the days when that phrase was being used in the courts in England it was in fact a horse-drawn carriage. The Clapham omnibus was the bus that went from Brixton to Clapham and it is now on display at the London Bus Museum for anybody who is interested in having a look at it. But this term was used to talk about a hypothetical ordinary and reasonable person (presuming that an ordinary person would also be a reasonable person), and it was offered to the courts in English law where it was necessary to decide whether a person had acted as a reasonable person would act – for example, in a civil action for negligence, say for somebody doing something wrong by not meeting proper standards in the practice of their professional duty. So the imaginary man on the Clapham omnibus would be reasonably educated, reasonably intelligent, but a nondescript person – an everyman – or a benchmark against which to test a reasonable view.

'It is said that the term was introduced into English law during the Victorian era, and it is still an important concept in British law. The origins of the term "Clapham omnibus" are rather vague, but the phrase was really first put into legal use and reported in a judgement in 1903 in an English court of appeal case. But the person who mentioned it attributed it to somebody who is said to have used it first as a junior counsel defending somebody in a case as far back as 1871. So "the man on the Clapham omnibus" became shorthand for an unidentified person at the back of a bus who could be loosely described as being reasonable. But recently, in or around 2014, the phrase was used again and indeed reviewed by the Supreme Court in the United Kingdom in a case where one of the judges said in his commentary: "the Clapham Omnibus has many passengers. The most venerable is the reasonable man, who was born during the reign of Queen Victoria but remains in vigorous good health. Amongst the other passengers are the right-thinking member of society, familiar with the law of defamation, the officious bystander, the reasonable parent, the reasonable landlord, and the fair-minded and informed observer, all of whom have had season tickets on this bus for many years. The horse-drawn bus between Knightsbridge and Clapham, which the original judges are thought to have had in mind, was real enough. But its most famous passenger, and the others I have mentioned, are legal fictions. They belong to an intellectual tradition of defining a legal standard by reference to a hypothetical person, which stretches back to the creation by reigning jurists of the figure of the bonus paterfamilias, which could loosely be described as 'the reasonable father figure'."

'The judge went on then to pull this theory apart a little, and concluded by saying that the behaviour of the reasonable man is not really established by the evidence of witnesses but by the application of a legal standard by the court: "The court may require to be informed by evidence of circumstances which bear on its application of the standard of the reasonable man in any particular case; but it is then for the court to determine the outcome, in those circumstances, of applying that impersonal standard."

'To support his argument, he said that in recent times some additional passengers from other countries have boarded the Clapham omnibus. And so you see here an example of terms that were applicable to times past becoming irrelevant in a cosmopolitan and changing society. It is interesting just to let you know that the expression has been incorporated into all sorts of other countries. For example, in Australia the Clapham omnibus expression has become "the man in the Bondi tram" (a now-disused tram route in Sydney, New South Wales) or "the man on the Bourke Street tram" (in Melbourne, Victoria). In Western Australia, the equivalent is "the man on the Prospector to Kalgoorlie", and in Hong Kong the equivalent expression is "the man on the Shaukiwan tram". And, believe it or not, here in Ireland, but more specifically in the Dublin area, we have been known to refer to "the man on the 46A".

'So, this gives you an idea of the lengths to which we have gone over time to try and find, when we are putting forward an argument for what would be an objective view of a fair outcome, the idea of this notional citizen who would represent all of those good qualities. I am sure, having listened to this, that you would agree with me that this is actually very hard to achieve, because you, from your experience in everyday life at school and elsewhere, would see lots of times when people would have differing views of what is fair and what is a good outcome.'

'Oh, well; I think that is very true, and the reason why there are so many fights, even in school, because people do not always see things the same way and get angry when their view of fairness is not shared by others or the teacher,' said Nova. The rest of the group agreed with her.

'Before we close our discussions in the first part of this project, I would like to bring the subject now to one which I am sure you know a lot about – that of bullying. I think it is important to talk to you about this because you can tell me lots about it from your experience at school.

But let us just summarise the legal aspect of this, because bullying does not stop at schools, let me tell you.

'There is bullying in workplaces, which causes huge amounts of people to be absent from work. Absenteeism, that is called, and indeed it causes so many difficulties that lots of employers set up training programmes, bringing in experts to talk about bullying and harassment, and do their very best to have avoidance and coping mechanisms built into their bullying policies, and human resource systems with zero tolerance for any kind of bullying or harassment at work.

'There are many definitions of bullying available, and some very good school programmes have simple ones that try to make it as identifiable as possible to children going through the upper parts of primary school and secondary school. Let us for the moment look at one school programme that I know of called the "Cool School Programme". It is important for you to be aware that there are many more programmes like that, and always ask in your school about the school programme for bullying if you have not been advised about it already, because every school must have a bullying policy – and not just in theory: they must have a process in place and the school management must be able to demonstrate how that policy works effectively to limit and address bullying in their school.

'So, bullying in the Cool School Programme is described as aggressive behaviour which is an abuse of power by an individual or group of individuals against others. It may be physical, verbal or psychological, and is usually deliberate and repeated – and that last word is very important for the definition in a case of alleged bullying, particularly in workplaces where people are making a complaint, because to demonstrate that it is bullying it is necessary to show the repetitive side of it.

'Bullying can often be racist, sexual or relational in nature, and those targeted often find it difficult to defend themselves against it. So, some kinds of bullying in school involve hitting or beating, kicking, pushing, pinching, tripping, choking, spitting, stealing, vandalising or damaging property. Verbal bullying could be name-calling, jeering, teasing, taunting, slagging, threatening, and daring others to do things they know to be dangerous or wrong. Psychological bullying would be excluding, isolating, demeaning, malicious gossip, spreading rumours, passing notes, using peer pressure to intimidate, scapegoating, setting others up for humiliation, threatening gestures or looks. Sexual bullying can be unwelcome sexual comments, unwelcome touching or spreading rumours about a person's sexual orientation. Racist bullying is discrimination, prejudice, comments about colour, nationality, ethnic or Traveller background.

'And then there is relational bullying, including manipulating relationships as a means of bullying. For example, this can be ignoring, excluding from the peer group, ostracising, spreading rumours, breaking confidences, huddling together to exclude others, talking loudly enough so the victim can hear their name being mentioned, demeaning dismissive looks, abusive messages, notes, letters, or drawings, abusive text messages, emails and phone calls.

'So, again I am sure I am merely adding to what you know already, or have heard about in school, but it is good just to write it down and to record it. Also, it would be very interesting to put this to Verity in France and to see how they cope with it in the schools and workplaces in her country.

'It is commonly accepted by experts who research and work in this area that adult help is almost always needed to solve bullying problems in the school place. Parents and teachers are ideally placed to influence attitudes and change behaviour, and the best way forward is for close co-operation between schools and parents if something arises.

'According to a number of studies in Ireland, only one in five students who were frequently bullied told their teachers. And only one in three told their parents. So, you can see from our conversation how important it is to give an overview of the information that would be needed for parents and students in a school about different aspects of bullying, that would help them identify the child who is being bullied or is bullying others, and to agree how to support them. I know that there are suggestions for parents in the Cool School guidelines on how to communicate effectively with teachers in schools on behalf of the children, and with their own children if that should come up.'

'It's difficult,' said Aver. 'Mumu, it's just so difficult. What do we need to do to stop disputes and to prevent them from turning into bullying? It worries me sometimes, because when you see your classmates in the playground being rude or teasing other people, how would you recognise this as bullying? They might take other people's toys or property. They might push them out of line when people are choosing teams for a game or for a project. They might not let them sit on the benches when people are talking after lunch. They might call them names, and that is very serious.'

'Yes,' said Lex, joining the conversation, 'it is. I think it is because of the way children will use anything to try and turn people against the child they have decided to be cruel about. If you listen to the things they say sometimes, you will agree that they are just plain silly. Let us think of examples to tell Mumu,' he said to Aver.

'The name-calling sometimes has "big" or "little" in front of it. It might try to make something nasty out of the fact that someone was wearing glasses as a reason to call them names or because they have black, brown, red or blonde hair. So it makes no sense really. I really do not understand it,' she said.

'People who want to be awful just add whatever words come into their heads to use it to hurt people. Things like, "Oh, look at him, he has brown hair" is about as silly as, "Look at her, she has brown eyes". So we really need to stop and think about the ways children can be cruel to other children,' added Rex.

'Yes,' said Nova. 'One way is to leave the person out of games. I see that happening so many times.'

'Well,' said Mumu, 'this is the time when the teacher's role is very important because they should be looking closely at the people who are likely to be bullied and at those who were being bullied in the past. And if they notice something like that, they should have a word with small groups and ask if they would like to discuss what they have noticed about the way some end up unhappy or fighting at playtime. The teacher can then put the idea to the groups, almost as if they were putting up a mirror to let them see a reflection of what their actions or words might appear like to them if they were on the receiving end.

'The teacher might then give them an opportunity to reflect on their discussion and come up with some suggestions about how they might find ways of avoiding disputes and fights. It would be more effective if lots of people could come up with suggestions about ways of avoiding clashes; then there would be more of a likelihood that the disputes could be avoided for a little bit longer, particularly as the young people would then know that the teacher had heard their descriptions of how things start to go bad.

'As we said before, we know that disputes, and even deep conflicts, can be resolved where the people involved can resolve long-standing differences. But the key ingredient is that the people want to find ways of making a plan for getting on with one another in a peaceful way, a plan that involves all sides showing respect for the others and that allows for differences in relation to some matters.

'Of course, if we can avoid disputes, fights and conflicts, then that is the best solution, is it not?

'How do you think we can go about that? Any ideas? Perhaps this is something you could have discussions about at any free discussion times in school, or at recreation periods where the teacher has encouraged you to talk about up-to- date topics and subjects if it is too wet or windy to go outside to the playground.'

At that point, Nova suggested, 'We would need to be good at observing the way children interact – that is, how they play and how they manage their friendships. Is that not true? We need to understand certain things about the way some children behave because that is the way they might always be if they are not given guidance.'

'That is so true,' said Mumu. 'And it is that understanding, that empathy that extends into people's behaviour, that helps us to help them to help themselves.

'There are so many ideas about how we can prevent bullying or manage it when it erupts. One of the catchphrases is "stop it soon" – the SIS motto. If somebody disagrees with another classmate, then if you notice that going on a lot you might be able to resolve the differences, but in spite of the fact that we are talking here about the possibility of intervening or attempting to help, we must bear in mind that the most important thing to do if you are being bullied, or see someone close to you being bullied, is to bring it to the attention of an adult, or someone in authority.'

Fourteen

Different courts – Latin the language of learning – the importance of listening and language – saying no to bullying and harassment

Mumu talked a little bit to the group about the different kinds of crimes against property and against the person, and just to refresh their memories she talked generally about the crime of stealing, as opposed to doing physical harm to somebody. She reminded them that they had talked about the symbols of law and about how we should deal with people who break the law in different ways, with an eye to keeping young offenders out of the criminal justice system, and how the sanctions and sentences should be different for those who are viewed as a danger to others.

'You can also think in terms of what we call simple claims, and for those we have developed what they call small claims courts where the value of the difference in the dispute between the people is of low level, so they need not go to the higher courts. Different courts have different "thresholds", as we call them, so a small claims court in one country might be for disputes about goods to the value of 5,000 or 10,000 euro or pounds or dollars, depending on the currency in that particular country.

'So, if there is a dispute between companies – commercial disputes, we would call those – there's a special commercial court. The bigger the claim, the higher the court, is the simplest way of looking at it. And then there is always, in a fair constitutional legal system, a layer of appeal above the original claim, so that you can appeal to a higher court and ultimately to the Supreme Court, if that is the highest appeal court – depending on the arrangements in different countries.'

'What do you mean by a commercial dispute, Mumu?'

'Well, a commercial dispute can be between companies or between people and a company. For example, if you have a contract – that is to say, a written or verbal agreement to buy something – and you pay for it but the seller does not deliver it to you, then you would take a claim against them. They would have to give your money back or give you the goods that you had originally ordered. If the court was satisfied that you did everything properly and that the seller failed or refused or neglected to keep their word and their side of the bargain, the seller would also have to pay the legal costs of the case, if you had given them every chance to give you the goods or to give you your money back.

'If somebody did some deliberate physical damage to another person or to their property, such as burglary or mugging, then these would be criminal actions, and if the person was found guilty, either by the judge having heard all of the evidence or by a judge with a jury testing the evidence, that person would have to go to prison or be fined a lot of money, or both.

'You may remember we discussed the different levels of proofs in cases, and that for a matter that is not a criminal one – that is, a civil claim – the proof in those cases is on the "balance of probability".'

Mumu then drove them down from the waterfall where they had enjoyed a pleasant picnic and decided they would head towards the coast to have a little walk along their favourite beach. They parked and set off towards the beach, where some people were swimming.

'Goodness,' said Aver. 'People are swimming in this weather!'

'Yes, people swim here in all weathers. Indeed it is true to say that a lot of the people who come here frequently swim every morning, and there is a famous swim here on St Stephen's Day, the day after Christmas Day, when many people come down and take a dive into the cold water. Sorry, I must correct myself, because everyone tells me that the water is not cold. Many of those people take the plunge in aid of some sponsored charity.'

Nova interrupted their laughter about people swimming at Christmas time and said: 'Mumu, about a week ago we were on a school trip and we noticed a very large sign saying, "No dumping here, it is illegal to dump material in this area". And one of the girls sitting next to me on the bus said, "That's a bit silly, because anyone could just drive past that sign and pretend not to know that it was there or not to have seen it. And then they would not be breaking the law, would they?"'

'Well, you raise a very interesting question, Nova, because your friend is not right, and indeed you might tell her about this sometime if you have the opportunity. There is an old maxim – a saying which goes, "Ignorance of the law is no defence".

'Now, I am going to give you some Latin here. That expression comes originally from the Latin expression *ignorantia juris non excusat,* which means ignorance of the law excuses not. Or, in the longer version, *ignorantia legis neminem excusat*, which means ignorance of the law excuses no one. This is a legal principle holding that a person who is unaware of the law may not escape liability for violating that law merely because he was unaware of its existence.

'The thinking behind this doctrine, if we can call it that, is that if ignorance were an excuse, a person charged with criminal offences, or some other legal claim, would merely say that he or she was unaware of the law to avoid liability, even if that person really did know about the law in question.

'Of course, you will say that it would be impossible for someone, even with a huge amount of legal training, to be aware of every law in operation, but this is the price paid to ensure that wilful avoidance cannot become the basis of escaping liability. Thus, it is very well understood that people who work in any area that goes beyond the law for ordinary people, such as running a very serious electrical plant or chemical factory, must make themselves aware of all the laws necessary to engage in that undertaking, and if they do not they cannot complain if they incur liability in the event of something serious going wrong and people being injured.

'Needless to say, in recent times some interpretations have tended to weaken this concept, particularly in civil law, where the difficulty of being informed of the existence of a law, considering the lifestyle of the average citizen, has to be taken into consideration. So the evaluation of a person's knowledge of the law is widely discussed as a topic, but it is generally accepted that people should have ample warning of laws changing, and in modern society law is widely available both in book form and on the internet, and commentary about new legislation is always heavily discussed in the media.

'Now,' said Mumu, 'I quoted some Latin to you there.

Latin is a very interesting language. It is referred to as a dead language, but in many respects Latin has always been the language of knowledge and learning and, just to summarise for you, it could be said that as science and medicine advanced through the ages, English writers took to coining words from Greek and Latin roots. Not so long ago, doctors always wrote their medical prescriptions in Latin, and there was always a presumption that people studying medicine or law had Latin as a subject. In fact, it was compulsory to have a qualification in Latin to start those courses.'

As they walked around the beach, Mumu shared a few of the more common Latin expressions that are met in everyday life. For example, the expression *bona fide*, which means "in good faith", implies sincere good intention, regardless of the outcome. For example, you could use the expression if you were discussing the Orange Grove case, where representatives from both of the communities adjoining the orange grove, who had been arguing for many years about the rights of access and ownership, decided to go into a form of dispute resolution called mediation, and both sides went in with a good intention of trying to find a resolution, so they approached the process in good faith or *bona fide*. It means that in human interactions there is a sincere intention to be fair, open and honest, regardless of the outcome of the interaction. In other words, you are giving something your best shot; you are not going to prejudge the outcome but, at the same time, you are going to give the process every opportunity of being a success.

'Some Latin phrases have lost their literal meaning over the centuries, but this is not the case with bona fide. It is still very widely used and interchangeable with its generally accepted modern day English translation of "in good faith". In fact, it is true to say that it is a very important concept within law and business and communications.

'Here is another one that you may have heard – caveat emptor. This means "let the buyer beware". In other words, it means that when we are purchasing something it is up to us to make ourselves aware of all the circumstances and have a good look before we buy, because we have to assume responsibility for having made the purchase after making many inquiries about the suitability and the quality of the product we were about to buy.

'Then we have another commonly used expression, *compos mentis,* which means having command of your mind, or "of sound mind". It is also used in the negative, *non compos mentis,* meaning "not of sound mind".

'I am sure you have often seen the two little letters "i.e." after something has been expressed. This is an abbreviation of *id est,* meaning "that is", in the sense of restating something that may not have been clear in the first instance. There is another expression that is used often in relation to the Children's Courts and to what we describe as Family Law, which are court cases about the break-up of a marriage and the care of the children. These cases are conducted in private, the opposite of "in open court", so it is said that such cases are held *in camera,* meaning literally "in a chamber", or in private.

'You might also have heard the expression in *loco parentis.* This is used to describe circumstances where somebody stands in the place of a parent or a guardian – for example, a teacher or somebody conducting a school tour where the children are in their charge. It is used to refer to a person or entity assuming the normal parental responsibility for a minor, given the circumstances. So this expression can be used in the case of schools, or other institutions that act in the place of the parents on a day-to-day basis.

'And then we have the expression *locus standi,* which

means "place of standing". This refers to the right of a party or a person to appear and be heard before a court. In other words, if someone is involved in some dispute, a friend might go there to be outside to help if they needed any support after the hearing, but they cannot stand up in the court and make any comment or contribution because they have no *locus standi* – they have no legal right to be heard before a court in relation to the matter.

'Then there is a very common expression which is used in relation to criminal cases particularly – *mens rea,* which means "guilty mind". It is one of the requirements for a crime to be committed, the other being *actus reus,* the "guilty act". So, for a crime to exist, there has to be the *actus reus,* the guilty act, and there has to be the *mens rea,* the guilty mind. This is essentially the basis for the notion that those without sufficient mental capability cannot be judged guilty of a crime, but that is a very complicated area, which we may discuss at a later stage.

'You will also have noticed, at the end of some writing or a list of things, *nota bene* or NB. That means "note well" – a term used to direct the reader to cautionary or qualifying statements regarding the main text.

'And I'll give you the last one now, because I am sure you are rather tired and eager to get home and to have dinner. So, the final one is *nulla bona,* which means simply "no goods". This is a notation made when a defendant, a person defending a claim against them, has no property or money available to be seized in order to comply with a judgement. So if somebody makes a claim against them and the judge imposes that claim, and the sheriff or other officer of the court goes to seize their property or their goods to pay the amount to the person who had made the claim, they would simply report back to the court *nulla bona,* meaning that there were no goods existing that could be used to provide for the order of the court.

'It might be a good idea if you took a note of any Latin expressions that you hear being used and perhaps put them in your project notebook and bring them back to one of our future discussions. You might also think about raising that as a question with Verity, to see if they use Latin in the same way in France.'

As she drove back to drop the group off, Mumu decided to speak generally about communications, and mentioned that in a negotiation or, indeed, any kind of debate, they probably noticed that people sometimes seem not to have really listened. Instead they wait their turn to speak and make their arguments.

'They seem to believe that the only way to convince their counterpart, or those to be persuaded, is to make their own case without hearing the opposing views. Negotiators' lack of real listening also means that they are more vulnerable if their counterparts use difficult tactics against them. Difficult tactics may include threats, lies, and false claims about lack of authority or conflicting commitments, or a host of other unpleasant behaviours intended to throw people off and curtail their bargaining power.

'So, faced with difficult tactics, we tend to have a very constricted vision, a limited vision of our options, like giving in, retaliating or walking away – none of which is conducive to a successful outcome or deal, which is so important to a continuing relationship, be that a personal one, a professional one or a commercial one.

'So, let me try to persuade you to take away from this part of our discussion the fact that listening well, or what is referred to in some of the mediation negotiation training courses as "active listening", really empowers people who are negotiating or trying to facilitate a dispute to maintain order in the process.

'When we talked about bullying, I mentioned to you

that to be classified as bullying, in the strict sense, it is required that the actions or behaviours complained about were repeated. Bullying is sometimes confused with harassment, which is similar to any form of unwanted conduct which has the purpose or effect of violating a person's dignity and creating an intimidating, hostile, degrading, humiliating or offensive environment.

'Bullying and harassment are very common causes of disruption and difficulty in places of work – indeed, as we have said before, in all places that people congregate – and it comes as a surprise to many that it can even be found in the common rooms of teaching institutions, universities, colleges and schools.'

The group expressed unified surprise at such a thought and appeared quite uncomfortable to hear that teachers could be involved in that with their colleagues.

'Bullying and harassment are similar in some respects, but also very different from a legal perspective, so it is helpful to be aware of what those differences are.

'With reference to Seamus Heaney's image of the conveyor belt of every generation that we discussed, you are on the conveyor belt of your generation, which involves a lot of engagement with the internet and social media platforms, so you should be fully aware of how the internet is used for bullying and for targeting very young people. We may have heard through the news, and even through personal experience of friends and others, about young people who have been victims. There have been tragic cases where young people have been targeted, victimised and tormented to great detriment in their lives. As you may know, sometimes, on what is described as the "dark web", people can contact young people and pretend to be people of the same age, but it turns out that they are actually predators, people who are looking for young victims to "groom" – that is to say, to pretend to befriend, try to insinuate into a relationship, with a view to being in contact with them and even encouraging them to meet up.

'I spoke earlier about the fact that there were lots of different kinds of anti-bullying programmes in schools and colleges, and another I heard of was called "Sticks and Stones". This was an anti-bullying process which encouraged the appointment of a support contact person or a designated contact person in either the workplace or the school, so that there were people to whom you could go if you had a problem, or if you were unsure about how you should go about making a complaint or bringing it to the attention of the right person.

'And, with that in mind, as we have already acknowledged, it's very important that anti-bullying policies must be clear. They must give information about where and how to seek help and, of course, the overriding policy on which all the experts agree is "nip it in the bud" – and there should be large posters in every school with that simple advice. So if you are on the receiving end of any bad behaviour in relation to any text messages or messages on social media platforms, you just say no; and sometimes saying no means not saying anything and not communicating at all with that person but reporting it to your parents and relevant teacher.

'We have spoken quite a lot about language, in passing, in our short journey down the road of discussing the law. It is true to say that language – the use of words – is central to clear and meaningful communications. A quote comes to mind from the American writer, Mark Twain, who wrote about the importance of choosing the "correct word" when he said, "the difference between the almost right word and the right word is really a large matter – it's the difference between the lightning bug and the lightning".

'Often people do not realise the importance of every word and how easily written information can be misconstrued by the reader's bias. There are many words, as we know, that have changed meaning over time. People use the words "cool" and "awesome", and forget that a few years ago the words may have been "groovy" or "fab" instead. Words can be addictive – such as saying "you know" or "like" repeatedly when speaking, which breaks up the sentences.

'Words change. Sometimes the whole meaning of a word changes or sometimes a trendy word simply goes out of style. Some words lose their appeal over time and unfortunately we become addicted to words that we use without even thinking about what their true meaning is. Someone told me recently about an exercise that was done with a group of young people who were shown a video re-enactment of a collision between two cars. In the course of that video a red car collided with a black car. The video played for about three minutes and the group went away and were told to come back in a week's time, when they were divided into two groups. One of the groups was asked what they recalled from the video when the black car collided with the red car, and they described what they recalled seeing. The other group was asked what they saw when the red car smashed into the black car. The group described in some detail how they recalled the accident and the windows being shattered in the crash. The use of the word "smashed" somehow brought to the listeners' minds the notion of the shattering of a windscreen and glass.

'I am just reminding you of the importance of listening skills and the importance of clarity in the words we use in our communications. So you need to be precise in your communication with Verity when you are explaining how the process of a legal system works in a common law jurisdiction, and when you are asking her to give you information about how similar topics are covered in her country.

'I am really looking forward to the next phase of this project when we meet to read Verity's responses and gain insights into the ways and means of arriving at fairness, justice and peace in her country.'

Mumu looked at the steady band of learners and found herself increasingly in awe of their commitment and endurance.

'It has been very interesting for me over the past few weeks touching on all of these subjects and I am impressed by all of you for being interested enough to stick with it. Thinking of Seamus Heaney's reference to every generation being on its own conveyor belt, I must say that my post-war, generation was full of hope that it would make things better, but I must say that I feel immense guilt at what I am handing on to you. It would not be an exaggeration to say that the world is in disarray and chaos at the moment. We have ethnic conflicts all over the world. People fleeing from poverty or persecution are risking their lives as refugees, amassing at foreign borders where there is no viable means of housing or feeding them, or providing them with medical treatment or education – not to mention a living. Climate change is not only threatening one weather disaster after another but is also the cause of conflict, as some countries deny that it is happening at all and will not sign up to agreed protocols to limit the damage of CO2 emissions and the pollution of our seas and fish stock with plastics. Some biologists and scientists will argue that there are not enough sustainable food resources to feed the growing population. With reference to our earlier discussion, our democracies are under threat from the manipulation of personal data through the misuse of social media platforms.

'All that I can say to all of you is that when we study history as a subject we find the books full of accounts of battles and wars, and for the first time, in the twentieth century, we have created institutions like the United Nations, with its Security Council, and groups such as the European Union, where we aim to keep dialogue open so that we can co-operate in relation to matters of common interest. We have good legal systems and processes to enable people to have access to justice and the protection of their rights. I do still feel guilty that I am handing over such a mess, but I point out to you the need to guard the processes underpinning all the systems that work for the protection of fundamental rights. The process is central; it should be sacrosanct, to be revered and respected. Do not let people tinker with the process, no matter what it is about. If it is designed to protect, it has to be followed even in the smallest examples. If it is the mediation process, if it is the way meetings are conducted, if it is the organising of elections, the treatment of people's complaints at work or elsewhere, the human resource practices at work, the handling of allegations of bullying and harassment, whatever is involved in the treatment of people and their rights should aim to have the high standards applied in our courts. If Aver ever did ask her teacher about corruption and share the information with you all, then you will know how much would be lost if our systems and processes were open to corruption.

'I look forward to going through the information from Verity when you receive it, and perhaps we will go to that Seamus Heaney exhibition on one of our future outings.'

'And maybe revisit some of our favourite places where we went?' laughed Aver.

'Yes, that is a good plan.'

About the Author

Paulyn Marrinan Quinn, Senior Counsel, was appointed as the first Insurance Ombudsman in Ireland, and thus began an interest in non-adversarial dispute resolution processes. She founded and directed a postgraduate programme in Trinity College, Dublin University, 'Conflict & Dispute Resolution Studies', where she taught as Adjunct Professor of Mediation & ADR Studies. She had the privilege of serving as the first Ombudsman for the Defence Forces in Ireland. She has written and produced documentaries for television and radio. She devised a radio series, 'Cases that Changed Peoples' Lives', reviewing a few defining court cases that changed things for the better for all of us. *What Does Law Mean, Mumu?* is her first book.

Acknowledgements

I wish to mention the valuable role played by all those who encouraged and supported me in making this book happen – too many to list all of them here. However, I must acknowledge a valued friend and mentor, Dr Eileen Doyle, who first suggested that I write the book. Eileen sadly passed away last year and her reputation as an academic, scholar, psychologist, consultant, and many other roles she held, was duly celebrated. In essence, she was committed to the advancement of education and nurturing self-belief and potential in young people. I would also like to thank Catherine McGlew of the Typing Department who painstakingly supported me along the road when I was trying to pull the drafts of the book together.